D1228860

CIVILIAN CONTROL
versus
MILITARY RULE

CIVILIAN CONTROL versus MILITARY RULE

Robert Previdi

Dear Mr. Ventruella:

My best regards.

Bob Previdi

HIPPOCRENE BOOKS
New York

Copyright © 1988 by Robert Previdi

All rights reserved, including the right to reproduce
this book or portions thereof in any form.

For information, address: Hippocrene Books, Inc.
171 Madison Avenue, New York, NY 10016

Library of Congress Cataloging-in-Publication Data

Previdi, Robert.
Civilian control versus military rule / Robert Previdi.
p. 192 34 × 51 cm.
Bibliography: p. 177
Includes index.
ISBN 0-87052-712-6
1. Civil supremacy over the military—United States. 2. Civil-military relations—United States. 3. United States. Dept. of Defense—Reorganization. I. Title.
JK558.P75 1988
353.6—dc19 88-21649
CIP

Printed in the United States of America.

American military theory has undergone much change since the founding of our nation, but not the idea that ultimate control rests with elected leaders and their appointed, politically accountable subordinates. It has been—and must continue to be—a principle of our form of government that professional military officers will not be held responsible for making essentially political decisions regarding the use of military force.

—John F. Lehman, Jr.
Former Secretary of the Navy

To these three people who have supported me in my life's goals.

My wife, Taimi Previdi
Richard S. Braddock
Joseph N. Mondello

CONTENTS

PREFACE

The next president of the United States, whether Republican or Democrat, will be faced with the immediate problem of recapturing the critical role of commander-in-chief of the armed forces. Legislation passed by Congress and signed by President Reagan, known as the Goldwater-Nichols Act, may have eroded and blurred the authority of the president by, for example, giving too much power to the secretary of defense.

Even more detrimental, however, has been the reorganization of the Joint Chiefs of Staff, making the chairman a single supreme military authority and sole military adviser to the president, the secretary of defense, and the National Security Council.

The Goldwater-Nichols Defense Department Reorganization Act became law on October 1, 1986. It is the most important piece of military legislation passed by Congress in the last forty years. It is also the most dangerous.

By creating one military czar, this legislation starts the nation down a road which can lead to a situation where, at best, the country is run more and more by the military and, at worst, where the country actually becomes more vulnerable to a military takeover.

This book is about civilian control of the military in the United States. By civilian control of the military I mean the control maintained by the president of the United States as head of the executive branch of our government and as commander-in-chief of our military forces. I also mean the secretary of defense, a civilian who runs the Department of Defense reporting to the president. We must face the fact that a president and a civilian secretary of defense are the top people running our military establishment—not simply because they are civilians, but precisely because, under our form of government, a civilian is best qualified to understand political policy, which must always form the basis of military strategy formation. This logic applies in peacetime, and as I will try to show is even more important in wartime.

I wrote this book because I believe the people's right to know is critical to the success of our country. Nothing is more dangerous and destructive than for the American people not to be fully informed. As Vietnam so clearly taught us, we can never go to war without the understanding, involvement, and approval of the American people. The only way the American public can be involved is for them to understand the pros and cons of each major issue.

Now for the first time in our history, one man—the chairman of the Joint Chiefs of Staff—becomes the nation's most powerful military officer. Few Americans know anything about the Goldwater-Nichols Act, which represents the first potential challenge to civilian control of the military in the history of the United States.

This book is not a criticism of the military. Too many books have been written which criticize the military while forgetting that in our form of government ultimate responsibility for the military belongs to our civilian leaders. The executive branch and Congress run and must continue to be responsible for running the nation's military establishment. Whether it be World War II, Korea or Vietnam, the responsibility for what happens—good or bad—belongs to our civilian leaders. There must never be a blur between the ultimate responsibility of our civilian leaders and the role of the military. In our form of government, the civilians decide what must be done, the military is responsible only for execution. This fact defines civilian control of the military.

Because of Vietnam, the attitude of our military has changed. This change is very important and very dangerous. The military is confusing political policy with military execution. What Vietnam did was to politicize the military. This is the worst thing that can happen in our form of government. And Congress, by passing the Goldwater-Nichols Act, furthers this reality by putting one military man in charge.

Civilian control of the military must never mean unqualified civilians dictating bad strategy to military leaders, as some high-ranking officers contended was the case in Vietnam. Civilian control must be seen in a much larger context. Civilians must be ultimately responsible for the effectiveness of our military establishment in peacetime and in wartime.

In our form of government, it's critical that the president and the secretary of defense be involved in the formation of military strategy. Only after strategy has been established can military execution be delegated to the military with oversight and ultimate responsibility still belonging to our civilian leadership. What our system must do is make clear the difference in roles between civilian leadership and the military while never forgetting that, no matter what happens, responsibility always belongs to the nation's civilian leadership in the executive branch and in Congress.

The Goldwater-Nichols Act starts this nation down a road which can lead, sometime in the future, to a situation where, at best, the nation is run more and more by military men and, at worst, the country can actually be taken over by the military.

I know these are very strong words. However, if I am right, then it is important that every concerned citizen read this book and then decide either to support the Goldwater-Nichols Act as passed or demand that it be significantly amended. There is no other power on earth, except the American people, who can get this dangerous and ill-conceived law changed.

Even key legislators like Congressman Les Aspin, Chairman of the House Armed Services Committee, who helped to get the legislation written and passed, admit the public knows nothing about it. This fact is a great failing and might very well explain why this bill got passed. I don't believe the American people would have allowed this to happen had they known about it. That's one of the main reasons why I have written this book. When explained to them, not one person I have talked to has any doubt about why the Goldwater-Nichols Act is wrong.

I write this book as a concerned citizen who has studied defense matters for over twenty-five years. Based on what I have learned, I believe very sincerely that the Goldwater-Nichols Act threatens the nation's freedom and safety. If you think about it, who has a greater obligation to write on this topic than a citizen who is concerned about his country?

This very important piece of legislation revolutionizes how the Department of Defense will be run and, ultimately, how effective our military forces will be in combat. In the end, whether we like it or not, our government is just a reflection of what we are as a people. If we don't like what we see, it is up to us to change it. The ability to get what we the people want changed is what makes our form of government surely more responsive than most others around the world.

As outlined in this book, the Goldwater-Nichols Act will not help us in wartime or in peacetime. The new legislation is, to a large extent, a reaction to what went wrong in Vietnam. Partly because of the Vietnam emphasis, the Goldwater-Nichols Act focuses on the period after World War II when the Department of Defense was formed. The legislation errs by not including the very important lessons of the Second World War, when our civilian leaders and our military leaders functioned so effectively together. I will try to show in this book why it is critical to use World War II as a model for trying to improve the way the Department of Defense is run.

Dr. Archie D. Barrett, a professional staff member of the House Armed Services Committee, made the point to me that the focus of the legislation was on what happened after World War II. This limitation has quite drastic consequences because it determined and limited the context in which the legislation was considered. It ultimately limited greatly the number of options Congress considered before deciding on what to include in the Goldwater-Nichols Act.

According to Dr. Barrett one of the objectives of the legislation was to increase the authority of the secretary of defense by keeping the secretary in the military chain of command under the president and by the secretary's having a stronger chairman of the Joint Chiefs of Staff to work with. I believe the new legislation does just the opposite. In actuality, it changes the relationship between the secretary of defense and the JCS chairman from one of natural allies to one of competitors for power. This situation will be increasingly destructive as, with time, the chairman becomes more powerful. Nothing can be more dangerous and destructive to the defense of the United States than to have the secretary of defense and the JCS chairman fighting for power. They must be allies.

Defense Secretary Weinberger wrote to me on October 20, 1987, to tell me that he was against the legislation but that he and Admiral Crowe, the current chairman, get along well. Here is what the Secretary wrote:

> Your concern over the alleged potential dangers of the Goldwater-Nichols Act, particularly the effect upon the position of the chairman of the Joint Chiefs of Staff, is understandable, and indeed we opposed the bill, but we do not think the Act will diminish civilian control of the military. An "all-powerful chairman" has not been created thus far.

I never worried about Secretary Weinberger being able to control the Defense Department because the momentum of civilian control has been such a powerful force over the last 200 years.

Secretary Weinberger is already gone while we have a new powerful force in the Goldwater-Nichols Act, which can be interpreted differently by different people. What we must ask ourselves is if this legislation has insured civilian control or threatened it?

For the first time in our history, we will have one military man who can totally control events. This can so easily lead to the greatest threat in our history to civilian control of the military. In addition, placing so much power with one military man from one service is the wrong way to improve the effectiveness of our military forces. At the end of this book I make seven recommendations that include the checks and balances needed to insure civilian control of the military while giving our military chain of command a more direct and logical structure.

I have tried to look at the world of the Department of Defense through the minds of many of the experts on this subject. I believe it is important for the concerned citizen to understand what different people think by reading what they have written. That is why this book contains many direct quotes. I have tried to pick those that effectively summarize important military thinking. Only by understanding the total picture seen through the minds of military authorities can we begin to intelligently form our own opinions. I have tried to make this book a funnel through which many books and thoughts may pass on their way to a comprehensive outline of military thinking in the United States. I have tried to make this book interesting, informative, and even exciting by focusing on important ideas and on decision making in the highest levels of our government. How we govern ourselves is important. The system we have has served us well. It will only continue to do so if every concerned citizen has the information needed to make informed judgments.

My special thanks to these people who helped me from beginning to end:
Ronne Bonder
General Chester V. Clifton
Lon Faller
Dr. Robert S. Hirschfield
Admiral Thomas H. Moorer
Philip Peppis
Glen C.H. Peny
General Matthew B. Ridgway

CHAPTER I

GOLDWATER-NICHOLS ACT

An Analysis of the Legislation

THE PURPOSE OF THIS BOOK IS TO ANALYZE THE POSSIBLE EFFECTS of the new Goldwater-Nichols Department of Defense Reorganization Act of 1986. No doubt about it, this is a major piece of legislation which Congressman Les Aspin, Chairman of the House Armed Services Committee, characterized as:

> . . . one of the landmark laws of American history. It is probably the greatest sea change in the history of the American military since the Continental Congress created the Continental Army in 1775.[1]

What must concern all Americans is how little coverage this drastic change in the civilian/military balance has received in the press. As a result, the American people are essentially unaware of the legislation and the short- and long-term implications it can have on our democracy.

Les Aspin, one of the key supporters, has also understood the importance of the Goldwater-Nichols Act and the lack of significant press coverage. On October 21, 1986, he said:

> While monumental changes have taken place with the Joint Chiefs of Staff, relatively nothing has appeared in the press because they just don't understand the significance of these changes.[2]

Starting on October 1, 1985, Senator Barry Goldwater (R-Az) and Senator Sam Nunn (D-Ga) delivered for six days a series of six speeches on the floor of the Senate. These very powerful speeches outlined in detail what they believed was wrong with our military establishment. They covered everything from the organization of the Office of the Secretary of Defense to what they thought was wrong with the Joint Chiefs of Staff to the issue of Congressional oversight. The one issue we thoroughly agree on is the need for a two-year defense budget. What I found surprising was the very powerful negative influence of former Chairman of the Joint Chiefs of Staff, Air Force General David C. Jones, versus the positive views of the then incumbent JCS Chairman, Army General John W. Vessey, Jr.

The efforts of Senators Goldwater and Nunn, along with Congressman Les Aspin and Congressman Bill Nichols, helped get this revolutionary legislation passed. After reading transcripts of the Senate and House hearings, I must admit I find it difficult to see how these legislators got from the problem they outlined in their speeches to the solution contained in the new legislation.

This legislation is a good example of insiders in Congress getting what they believe is right without the knowledge of or approval of the American public. The press really has let the country down by not sufficiently covering this most important piece of military legislation.

If Congress is right with their fundamental assumption that jointness—the joint action of all of the services working together—is the most effective way to solve all military problems, then all is well. However, if they are wrong, it could have dangerous consequences far beyond our imagination. It seems logical to have a balance between the importance of jointness versus having strong individual services.

My belief is that the bill has not been put in the historical perspective covering the period from World War II to the present. It has not considered what legislation does by changing the delicate balance within the Joint Chiefs of Staff—nor has it solved the essential problem of the unmanageable dispersion of authority and responsibility in our military services. It has focused narrowly on what might be improved by this legislation while not thoroughly considering the possible negatives it has created. It also has not considered the reality of nuclear weapons and the fact that in world affairs today, particularly because of modern communications, political policy, more than ever, must determine not only military strategy but often military operations as well.

The primary people who pushed reorganization so forcefully were Senator Barry Goldwater, Chairman of the Senate Armed Services Committee; Senator Sam Nunn, Ranking Minority Member of the Senate Armed Services Committee; Congressman Les Aspin, Chairman of the House Armed Services Committee; and Bill Nichols, Chairman of the House Investigations Subcommittee.

These dedicated men felt very strongly, based on their extensive experience and knowledge, that the nation's military organization needed drastic revisions to improve both efficiency and, particularly, effectiveness.

The areas they believed had to be changed were:

• *Operational failures and deficiencies.* Poor inter-service coordination during the Vietnam conflict, the Iranian hostage rescue mission, the Beirut barracks bombing, and even the intervention on Grenada, suggested deficiencies in the planning and preparation for employment of U. S. military forces in times of crisis.

• *Acquisition process deficiencies.* Cost overruns, stretched-out development and delivery schedules, and unsatisfactory weapons performance have been frequent criticisms of the acquisition process.

- *Lack of strategic direction.* The strategies and long-range policies of the Department of Defense do not appear to be well formulated and are apparently only loosely connected to subsequent resource allocations.
- *Poor inter-service coordination.* The programs of the individual military services do not appear to be well integrated around a common purpose that clearly ties means to goals.[3]

In many ways, the Goldwater-Nichols Act revolutionized how the military operates. My focus is principally on that part of the legislation where civilian control of the military is at issue; the points where our civilian leaders in the executive branch, principally the president and the secretary of defense, determine policy and then the crucial points where political policy must be used to establish military strategy. This, then, is the strategy that must be implemented by our military services. The critical questions or issues to consider with the new Goldwater-Nichols Act are:

- Will it improve military efficiency and effectiveness by greatly increasing the power of the chairman of the Joint Chiefs of Staff and by also increasing the power of the unified and specified joint combatant commanders* around the world?
- Has it, in fact, created a situation where the president and the secretary of defense can be blindsided by a JCS chairman who gives them only the information that best serves the chairman's objectives? This undesirable situation can result from a chairman who is cunning and smart or from a chairman who is not overly competent. Therefore, do we run the risk that over time even overall policy will be determined directly or indirectly more and more by the military?

*Unified combatant command—a military command that has broad, continuing missions and is composed of forces from two or more military services.

Specified combatant command—a military command that has broad, continuous missions and is normally composed of forces from a single service.

• Is it right to assume, as this bill does, that the concept of joint military operations alone should dominate all thought and decision making? To downgrade the individual services so drastically, as this legislation does, will have very serious future consequences. This narrow approach will not serve the president, the secretary of defense, or the country well.

It is my view that by greatly decreasing the power of the individual service chiefs and the civilian service secretaries, which I believe will be one of the results of the new legislation, we will without question begin the process of jeopardizing civilian control over the military. Once the JCS chairman becomes dominant in running the military bureaucracy, civilian control of the military will become increasingly difficult to maintain. The following is an outline of what the new legislation includes.

Increased Powers of the Chairman of the Joint Chiefs of Staff

The chairman of the Joint Chiefs of Staff is the principal military adviser to the president, the National Security Council (NSC), and the secretary of defense.[4]

We now move from the old system where the president and the secretary of defense received advice on an equal basis from *all* the services to one where one man from one service becomes the single most powerful military leader in our history. The success of our whole system of government is based on checks and balances. Civilian control of the military also has been based on this important principle. The JCS chairman is now in a position to dominate the other service chiefs, the service secretaries, and the unified and specified war-fighting commanders around the world.

In his thoughtful June 1984 article in *The New York Times*, former chairman of the Joint Chiefs Lyman L. Lemnitzer, wrote:

> The best way to give civilian leaders balanced military advice is by using the talents and broad experience of the military chiefs of all services. Each knows his own service; each is an expert in his field. Our present organization provides the checks and balances that moderate extreme views.[5]

In his 1946 testimony before the Senate Committee on Naval Affairs, the relatively unknown, brilliant leader of the U. S. Navy during World War II, five-star Fleet Admiral Ernest J. King, said:

> The strength of the Joint Chiefs of Staff lies in the combined knowledge possessed by the individual members and in the checks and balances that tend to prevent domination by any one person.[6]

The Goldwater-Nichols Act does the opposite. It begins the process of putting exceptional power in the hands of one military man. Congressman Les Aspin said, "We are creating a military structure 'single led and prepared to fight as one regardless of service.' "[7] This concept might sound good until we ask ourselves what its implications are. Having one military leader as the boss may lead to military efficiency, and even that is questionable, but it could be at the expense of effective policy formation and civilian control of the military. As General Matthew B. Ridgway wrote:

> The persistent contention by some of our own private citizens as well as military men that wars, once started, should be shaped and conducted solely by the military indicates that, improbable as it may seen, and incompatible as it is with our whole way of life, military dominance over our affairs "could happen here."[8]

In addition I contend that the atomic bomb necessitates that, more than ever, civilian authority not stop at the political/strategic stage but run under certain circumstances all the way through to include operations. This point is made later on, particularly in the section dealing with the Cuban Missile Crisis of 1962.

> *The new legislation allows the president to reappoint the JCS Chairman to a third two-year term.*[9] (However, in time of war, there is no limit on the number of reappointments.)

This seems like a mild change except that it again separates the chairman from the other chiefs. It is another way by which the chairman can enforce his authority and silence the chiefs or get them to do what he wants at the expense of alternative points of view going to the president, the secretary of defense, and the National Security Council. The end result of this new reality is that once the chairman controls what information gets to the president and the secretary of defense, civilian control and effective policy formation are both at risk. Of course, we have a different type of problem if the chairman of the Joint Chiefs is not particularly qualified. Both constitute dangerous situations for the country.

A new president can ask for the resignation of every political appointee in the executive branch. This freedom, however, does not easily apply to the JCS chairman or to the other members of the Joint Chiefs of Staff. Their terms are fixed by law so an incoming president cannot make changes without having a very good reason for doing so. It is critical in any administration for the president to have an officer he has confidence in. That is why the length of service of each these officers—particularly the chairman—is very important.

Even during a wartime crisis situation, the president is limited to two terms because of the Twenty-second Amendment to the Constitution. So no matter how great the threat, we would have to switch from an experienced leader to one with no experience no matter what the people would want.

The JCS chairman, on the other hand, can serve indefinitely during a wartime situation. What could be worse than to change a president while leaving the military leader in place during a time of emergency? The situation where either one is forced to leave while the other stays is illogical and dangerous.

Consider the consequences of having a powerful chairman already in office when a new administration comes into office. What it means is that the president and the secretary of defense must start their administrations by competing for control with one powerful force, the chairman. This situation must never be allowed to happen. It is too dangerous.

Responsibilities of the JCS Chairman

Another feature of this bill transfers responsibility for the duties currently performed by the corporate Joint Chiefs of Staff to the chairman and expands these duties to specify these new statutory duties to the chairman of the Joint Chiefs of Staff. Some of the points include:

- Strategic direction—Assist the president and the secretary of defense in providing for the strategic direction of the armed forces.
- Strategic planning—Prepare strategic plans, including plans that conform with resource levels projected by the secretary of defense.
- Prepare joint logistics and mobility plans.
- Perform net assessments to determine the capabilities of the armed forces of the United States and its allies as compared with those of their potential adversaries.
- Advise the secretary of defense on the critical deficiencies and strengths in force capabilities that are identified during the preparation of contingency plans and their effect on meeting national security objectives.

• Establish and maintain a uniform system of evaluating the readiness of the unified and specified commands.

• Advise the secretary of defense on the extent to which the services' budget proposals conform with the priorities of strategic plans and of the unified and specified commanders.

• Submit to the secretary of defense alternative budget proposals in order to achieve greater conformance with the priorities of strategic plans and of the unified and specified commands.

• Recommend to the secretary of defense a budget proposal for activities of each unified and specified command.[10]

With this kind of all-inclusive authority, we risk the possibility that the chairman of the Joint Chiefs can become stronger in establishing policy, strategy, and operations than even our civilian leaders. Nothing could be more dangerous for the United States of America. As Admiral King put it:

> We have only to look around us to be aware of countries where control of the armed forces decides control of the government.[11]

As outlined in the recommendations chapter, there are simpler and more logical ways to increase both the usefulness of the JCS chairman and the way in which the entire Defense Department is managed. What the Goldwater-Nichols Act does, in essence, is replace the wisdom of all the services with that of one all-knowing officer from one service. Lawrence Korb warned us when he wrote:

> Even powerful civilian leaders find it difficult to overrule unanimous military opinions. Without the existence of the separate services, military opinions would always be unanimous.[12]

Unanimous decisions coming from the military are a threat to effective decision making and, ultimately, to civilian control of the military. With the JCS chairman making all decisions, everything automatically becomes unanimous, dangerous, and limited in scope.

Vice Chairman

The Goldwater-Nichols Act also created the new position of vice chairman to the chairman of the Joint Chiefs of Staff. This change could be considered logical if the vice chairman were simply there to assist the chairman. It is my belief that we are creating a whole new expensive bureaucracy by increasing the power of the chairman of the Joint Chiefs and by making the vice chairman the number two man in our military establishment. This officer actually outranks all the individual service chiefs. The consequences here are enormous. And, illogical as it may sound, the vice chairman is not even a member of the Joint Chiefs of Staff. I can think of no more powerful and stunning way to permanently downgrade the Joint Chiefs of Staff as a body and as individual heads of their services.

Creating the new vice chairman position further increases the overall dominance of the chairman's authority. Most important, it does this at the expense of the other members of the Joint Chiefs because, for one thing, the new vice chairman outranks them. This reality significantly downgrades the role and value of the individual service chiefs including their staffs. Even former army chief of staff General Edward C. Meyer, who was one of the first leaders who recommended changing the Joint Chiefs, admitted that:

> The addition of this vice chairman would degrade the position of the service chiefs.[13]

Having a vice chairman will not improve joint military operations but will, in fact, do just the opposite. To believe that a joint staff, serving under a vice chairman, can ever duplicate the capability and expertise of the individual service staffs is illogical. I don't believe the men who pushed for this new legislation truly understood the enormity of what they have done. Here is what the legislation says:

> *The vice chairman, while so serving holds the grade of general or, in the case of an officer of the navy, admiral, and outranks all other officers of the armed forces except the chairman.*[14]

On this point former vice chief of staff, General Bruce Palmer, Jr., has written:

> Only one individual, the chairman, should exercise the authority and assume the responsibilities that go with that position. Moreover, the service chiefs should not be relegated to a position of influence below that of a deputy chairman.[15]

Making the vice chairman the number two person in the military proves beyond doubt that from now on the positions of army and air force chiefs of staff and the chief of naval operations plus the commandant of the Marine Corps will be downgraded in effectiveness and, I believe, will become increasingly ceremonial. Former Navy Secretary, John F. Lehman, said to me, "The Chiefs will not become ceremonial—they already are."[16] How this reality will increase the effectiveness of our military forces is a mystery to me.

Here is what Admiral William J. Crowe, Jr., the current Chairman of the Joint Chiefs of Staff, has said about the position of vice chairman:

> I personally concur with promoting the director* to four stars and designating him as a "vice-chairman." To me this is a logical step toward sharing the chairman's duties, thereby permitting him to manage his time better and strengthening management of the joint staff. I do,

*This refers to the current Director of the Joint Staff of the Joint Chiefs of Staff.

> however, subscribe to the present arrangement where the chiefs of services act in the chairman's stead during his absence from Washington and assume this responsibility for a set period. My short time in office has convinced me that both the services and the JCS benefit from the chief's experience as acting chairman.[17]

Most authorities would agree—the director of the Joint Staff does not have adequate authority over the hundreds of individuals he is responsible for managing. For the Goldwater-Nichols Act to have fixed this problem would have been sensible. Similarily, as Admiral Crowe outlined, it would have made sense to recognize the importance of the director's position as head of the Joint Staff and make it a four-star position. Then it would have been logical to designate the director of the Joint Staff as "deputy chairman." The difference between having a vice versus a deputy chairman is quite significant.

The vice chairman's position will end up being nothing but a messy bureaucratic intrusion. I don't see, for example, how the new vice chairman will help to improve the working relationship and effectiveness between the Joint Staff and the individual service staffs. That is why the new, total dominance of joint thinking, created by the Goldwater-Nichols Act, will in time lead to another change. This change will have the service staffs merged into the Joint Staff reporting to the JCS chairman. His power will then be so dominant as to insure the demise of the individual service chiefs. To make the Goldwater-Nichols momentum complete, all you need to do is create one service under the JCS chairman whose title might switch to military chief of staff or, worse, military commander-in-chief.

Admiral Crowe rightly did not conceive of the vice chairman outranking the other members of the Joint Chiefs of Staff—few people did. This drastic change, under the Goldwater-Nichols Act, will radically weaken the entire structure of the Joint Chiefs of Staff. It is a dangerous mistake with far-reaching consequences.

The degree of dominance of the chairman and the vice chairman over the other service chiefs is clear when reading the part of the legislation concerning the National Security Council. It says:

> *The chairman (or in his absence the vice chairman) of the Joint Chiefs of Staff may, in his role as principal military adviser to the National Security Council and subject to the direction of the president, attend and participate in meetings of the National Security Council.*[18]

The vice chairman represents the chairman at National Security Council meetings and yet, as I mentioned above, he is not even a member of the Joint Chiefs of Staff. This means the Joint Chiefs will have no involvement or direct knowledge of political policy formation; it will only be the chairman and the vice chairman who matter.

The JCS Chairman and the Commanders Around the World

The new bill greatly strengthens the authority of the ten military commanders around the world. It is a good idea to increase the authority of the field commanders downward in their joint organizations. It is not a good idea when it begins the process of limiting the control the president and the secretary of defense have on determining political policy/strategy and military operations. The other negative is when the increased power of the combatant commanders is achieved at the expense of the service chiefs and even the secretaries of the army, navy and air force.

Here are some additional details of the new law:

> *The chain of command to a unified or specified combatant command runs: (1) from the president to the secretary of*

defense; and (2) from the secretary of defense to the commander of the combatant command.[19]

This is fine and is essentially what we have had; however, this next point is crucial.

The president may direct that communications between the president or the secretary of defense and the commanders of unified and specified combatant commands be transmitted through the chairman of the Joint Chiefs of Staff.[20]

Inserting this new all-powerful JCS chairman more firmly between the secretary of defense and the joint commanders is tricky business indeed.

What we must always make absolutely certain is that the president and the secretary of defense have the information coming to them that enables them to control events. To have a system that allows one military man, the JCS chairman, to determine what gets to the secretary is contrary to civilian control of the military as outlined in our Constitution. Under the current system, it will become increasingly difficult for the president and the secretary to have open and meaningful communication with the CINCs (commanders-in-chief). More and more the CINCs will be dominated by the JCS chairman. This will result in the secretary being faced with a single voice coming from the military. Under this condition it essentially will be impossible for any secretary of defense to do his job of effectively serving the president's needs. We cannot let this dangerous situation become ingrained in our system of government. It is too dangerous.

This new arrangement makes the chairman the key person at the expense not only of the secretary of defense, but also the other chiefs as well and to some extent the service secretaries. We cannot risk a system that puts this kind of power and control in the hands of one unelected military man. The Department of Defense is, by far, the largest and most powerful branch of government. Under civilian control it works to defend our freedom; without civilian control it becomes the biggest threat to our freedom. This fact must never be forgotten because, ultimately, all our freedoms depend on civilian control of our military.

In a February 6, 1958, letter to Defense Secretary Neil S. McElroy, General Matthew B. Ridgway put it brilliantly:

> The alternative, frequently proposed, and in recent years generally employed, of vesting one man in uniform with authority to deny this access, and to represent before the highest executive and legislative councils of the Nation that he speaks authoritatively for all the services, is to court disaster. Sooner or later, if such a practice were followed, we would find in an encumbent of such a position a combination of arrogance, stubbornness, disregard for law, and thirst for power which would override all opposition from below and usurp from above additional authority it was never intended he should exercise.[21]

Under the new law the chairman can manipulate information so as to blind-side and control our civilian leaders with no risk of being challenged by the other chiefs. Over time the chairman's control of the chiefs will be total. Even though the new bill allows the chiefs to appeal to the president and the secretary of defense, in reality, this will rarely happen. Military men are taught to follow orders and this new legislation not only sends the wrong message to the chiefs, but also will over time make them ambiguous firgureheads with no function except to follow the chairman's orders.

Former JCS Chairman Thomas H. Moorer agrees. The increased power of the chairman will be at the expense of the other chiefs. He uses the word "degrading" to describe the result. He writes that additional authority goes to the chairman, "while degrading that of the service chiefs."[22]

> *The president may assign duties to the chairman to assist the president and the secretary of defense in performing their command function.*[23]

Can you imagine anything more dangerous? Here is another example of where the chairman can control his bosses and become a military czar. Think also of what could happen if the chairman is not overly competent. Either way, the country loses. No matter how efficient it may sound to have one military man dominate the command function, it is wrong. The individual chiefs must be a part of the process. In fact, part of the problem is that the chiefs have already been downgraded when compared to World War II period. Lawrence Korb wrote:

> Since 1947, the chiefs have lost and never regained their World War II heights when within themselves they combined command and planning and maintained direct access to and the confidence of the president.[24]

Consider further the position a chairman, who is already in office, would be in when a new administration comes into office. He will have the momentum of experience and military dominance on his side and this will be increasingly so over time. A new president and a new secretary of defense would have to get their power back—and God forbid if we would be at war at that time. Nothing in the history of our country could be more dangerous.

> *The secretary of defense may assign to the chairman of the Joint Chiefs of Staff responsibilities for overseeing the activities of the combatant commands.*[25]

What this unique authority does is risk giving the chairman *total* control of the military. Now the ten worldwide commanders will be answerable to only one person—the chairman. The balance previously supplied by the need for involving all the services will be gone. We can definitely expect the chairman's strength to get greater and greater—there is no other possible direction. Therefore, the chairman, with his new power, in time becomes potentially so powerful as to dominate both the secretary of defense and the president. Once started, this kind of threat will be difficult to stop. The executive branch and Congress have been able to stay in control because the system we were working under had the needed checks and balances. This is no longer the case. Admiral King said:

> I am strongly of the opinion that it is unwise to create by statute a situation which places full control of the armed forces in the hands of any one man, civilian or military, other than the president.[26]

Another major point of the legislation:

> *Specifies that the JCS chairman is to serve as the spokesman for the unified and specified commanders, especially on their operational requirements.*[27]

Now the ten worldwide commanders would have no need to be concerned about the chiefs of their services. What this does indirectly is dangerously reduce civilian control of the military by making the other military chiefs relatively powerless. In fact, the only power they could possibly have is through the chairman. The idea that they can, as the old and new law allows, still go over the chairman to the president and the secretary of defense defies bureaucratic reality. Even under the old system, consider how rarely this actually happened. The facts are the old legislation did allow the chairman to have great power but, fortunately, only the amount his civilian superiors wanted him to have.

In my view the issue of control is what people like former JCS Chairman Air Force General David C. Jones didn't like. Unfortunately, this narrow thinking and a misreading of history convinced Congress that the chairman needed greatly increased power in order to be effective. What was not foreseen was that the chairman's increased power, under the Goldwater-Nichols Act, would be at the expense of civilian authority. In contrast to General Jones, former JCS Chairman Thomas H. Moorer has written:

> In my view, the chairman already has all the power and authority he wishes to take.[28]

The degree of power the chairman has must flow directly from the president and the secretary of defense. This is precisely what the Goldwater-Nichols Act threatens. For example, it is almost unanimously agreed that General John W. Vessey, Jr., was a superb chairman because he had the confidence of the president, the secretary of defense, Congress and, perhaps most important, the other chiefs. In contrast to General Jones, the old system, although not perfect, did not restrict General Vessey's effectiveness. As my recommendations will outline, we can improve the system while also insuring civilian control.

The critical point is that the degree of authority the chairman has must flow directly from the president and the secretary of defense following the orders of the president. To have it any other way creates points of dangerous conflict between civilian authority and the military with risky, long-term implications for the country.

Said another way, the chief of naval operations, the chiefs of staff of the army and air force and the commandant of the Marine Corps can be isolated by the chairman from the president and the secretary of defense. This has happened even under the old system. For example, it happened when Admiral Arthur W. Radford was chairman and determined in 1954 to commit American forces to Southeast Asia. In order to present the opposite view to President Eisenhower, General Ridgway actually had to risk his military career. Admiral James L. Holloway, former chief of naval operations, said:

> As the power of the chairman expands and the supporting staff is increasingly subordinated to reflect only the chairman's views, the secretary of defense and the president become isolated from all military points of view but that of the chairman. So civilian authority, instead of retaining command, in effect abrogates that authority to the chairman of the Joint Chiefs of Staff.[29]

Another specific of the legislation:

Specifies that the JCS chairman manages the Joint Staff; the chairman is to prescribe the duties and staffing procedures of the Joint Staff.[30]

This may lead to greater efficiency, but it also greatly increases the power of the chairman at the expense of the other members of the Joint Chiefs of Staff, the other service secretaries and, ultimately, civilian control of the military.

Admiral Holloway said:

> It is true that the decision-making process could be streamlined, but only at the expense of eliminating the deliberation of considerations and alternatives which ultimately lead to better decisions.[31]

In addition, based on its belief that joint thinking solves all problems, the Goldwater-Nichols Act confused the important difference between the Joint Staff and the service staffs. Under the current legislation the JCS chairman runs the Joint Staff. The all-important service staffs, critical to the overall effectiveness of our military capability, do for the moment remain under the individual service chiefs. Most high-ranking officers believe the power of the individual chiefs is secure as long as they run the service staffs. I am not so sure. How this turns out will be an interesting power struggle between the JCS chairman, the service chiefs and the service secretaries.

If the individual service chiefs lose this one, they are finished. How this whole issue turns out will have serious consequences for our nation. Said simply, the Congress has not understood what it has done by passing the Goldwater-Nichols Act. General Bruce Palmer, Jr., wrote:

> . . . it means that only the service staffs possess the technical expertise in all matters affecting their respective services—force structure, logistic support, detailed knowledge of their ships, aircraft, and weapons systems, and so forth. This means that the Joint Staff cannot

> possibly duplicate the know-how existing in each service staff. This is why it is essential that the service staffs participate in the joint process functioning under the JCS.[32]

When he wrote this in 1984, General Palmer could never have foreseen how powerful the new law would make not only the JCS chairman but also the vice chairman as well. The delicate balance between the chairman, on one hand, and the individual chiefs, on the other hand, has drastically switched in favor of the chairman. In other words the other members of the Joint Chiefs will be essentially removed from the process. They will no longer be primary advisers, heads of their service, or even indirectly in the chain of command—they will be sideline players with no power to question decisions or to develop alternatives. Some critics have said the Joint Chiefs of Staff have not been giving sharp advice to the president and the secretary of defense. A secretary like Harold Brown would agree; in contrast, Caspar Weinberger would disagree. But the fact remains that now our civilian leaders will receive the definitive advice of one military man—the all-knowing JCS chairman. Heaven help us.

Admiral Moorer wrote:

> The chairman of the Joint Chiefs of Staff's authority to select and manage the Joint Staff . . . is the best way to ensure that we have a group of staff officers who know little or nothing about operations and combat. During this century the Germans have tried this procedure twice and their box score so far is won 0, lost 2.[33]

To put events into historical perspective, here is a brief review of what the Constitution says about our military and civilian control of the military.

The Constitution and the Military

The issue of how the United States of America would deal with control of the military goes back to the Constitution. What the men who wrote the Constitution wanted to avoid was making the executive branch too strong, as had been the case in Europe. Yet they knew it was not practical or safe to give the legislative branch exclusive control over the military.

Ultimately, it was decided that the executive branch—namely, the president—should be the leader of the military, while the legislative branch—the Congress—had the power of the purse and the power to declare war.

How much power does the president really have as commander-in-chief and what exactly is the role of Congress? Is the power to declare war just a passive issue that formalizes an action already taken by the president, or did the founding fathers mean for the Congress, as representatives of the people, to decide when we go to war, with the president taking over, as commander-in-chief, after war has been declared?

In "The Scope and Limits of Presidential Power," Dr. Robert S. Hirschfield formulated the issue:

> The president is "commander-in-chief of the army and the navy of the United States." But does this make him only the nation's "first general and admiral," as Alexander Hamilton insisted, or does it empower him to use the armed forces in such a way as to commit the nation to war?[34]

So the framers of the Constitution split the authority to control the military between the president and Congress. They decided that the president would be "Commander-in-chief of the army and navy of the United States." Congress, on the other hand, ended up with the formidable powers:

To declare war

to raise and support armies

to provide and maintain a navy

to make rules for the government and regulation of the land and naval forces

to make all laws that shall be necessary and proper for carrying into execution the foregoing powers.

With this split in authority, the issue of how power would be specifically shared has been fought over for the last 200 years. The conflict is sure to continue. Sometimes the president will have the upper hand, sometimes Congress, with public support ultimately being the determining factor of which branch will be stronger at any particular time. Robert Hirschfield said:

> Neither Lincoln nor Roosevelt could have acted with such spectacular independence in meeting the challenges confronting them had they lacked solid public support, but with that support they could push their powers to the limits of constitutionality and beyond.[35]

Like those of the presidency, the tools of the Congress under the Constitution can be very powerful. The power of the purse is a very interesting control. When used with decisiveness and with public support, as was done at the end of the Vietnam war, it gives Congress the power to control the military and the executive branch almost to whatever extent it wants. So if Congress chooses to use its power, it can essentially immobilize the power of the president as commander-in-chief.

The other brilliant point in the Constitution is not allowing the executive branch nor the military establishment to control the money. Giving the Congress the power of the purse was a brilliant idea. As George Mason put it: "The purse and the sword ought never to get into the same hands."[36]

Civilian control of the military by both the executive and legislative branches is clearly one of the most brilliant elements of our Constitution. The great strength of our system is that the conflict over who controls the military is between the executive branch and the Congress, both civilian authorities representing the people. The fight is not between civilian versus military authority. I believe the Goldwater-Nichols Act jeopardizes this critical safeguard that has served us so well for over 200 years.

What the Goldwater-Nichols Act can do is change the struggle for control of the military from one civilian branch of government versus another to a struggle between two civilian branches of government, the executive branch and Congress, versus the military establishment. Once started, this fundamental change in our government is a dangerous path to start down. Nothing in the new legislation makes it worth the risk.

The Goldwater-Nichols Act is, in my view, a poorly thought-out piece of legislation. It does not sufficiently consider our military history since 1941 nor what the possible long-term consequences can be of so drastically increasing the power of the chairman of the Joint Chiefs of Staff.

History of the Last Forty-Seven Years

This section of the book explores some of the history of what has happened, starting with the administration of Franklin D. Roosevelt, which has affected the civilian versus military balance within our government. The objective is to place the Goldwater-Nichols Act within the context of modern American political and military history.

Traditionally, during peacetime, the congressional power of the purse has been a major factor in how the military has been managed. During wartime, the cost is relatively unimportant while the need for quick unified decisions dominates, so the president becomes the primary force. This was clearly evident during World War II.

One factor—the discovery of the atomic bomb—has, in my view, altered the traditional balance between the executive branch and Congress, by necessity, in favor of the president. The president can no longer focus only on what he wants to accomplish politically. Therefore, military strategy and even implementation are increasingly the president's concerns. Korea, the Cuban Missile Crisis, and Vietnam are clear examples of this reality.

To make my point, I am going to compare Roosevelt: as a military leader during World War II; with President Harry S. Truman during Korea; with how President Dwight D. Eisenhower handled the military; with President John F. Kennedy during the Cuban Missile Crisis of 1962; and finally, with Vietnam. The focus is on the president as the civilian head of the military and shows why the new legislation can result in weakening the president's critical role as commander-in-chief.

Premise

Even though he was dealing with one of the greatest threats in our history, President Roosevelt was the last president who made a sharp division between the need to control overall political/strategic policy while having operations delegated to the military. The following chapters outline how nuclear power, other modern military weapons, and rapid communication have forced each succeeding president, since Roosevelt, to more thoroughly control military strategy and implementation.

CHAPTER II

WORLD WAR II

Franklin D. Roosevelt and the Military

DURING WORLD WAR II, CONGRESS GAVE THE MILITARY whatever it asked for. There never was any question, once war was declared, that whatever key military leaders, like Army Chief of Staff George C. Marshall or Chief of Naval Operations and Commander-in-Chief of the U. S. fleet Ernest J. King, wanted, they got. Congressional control through the power of the purse was never an issue.

So Congress declared war, the president served as commander-in-chief of the military, and the Joint Chiefs of Staff, who were actually not legally established until 1947, had enormous power. There was absolutely no blurring of authority or conflict between the executive branch, the Congress, and our military forces. The clear defender of civilian control of the military was President Franklin D. Roosevelt.

President Roosevelt kept control of the military primarily through General George C. Marshall and Admiral Ernest J. King, the two key military leaders of the war. The president knew that these two men were his means of controlling military affairs and getting anything he wanted done anywhere in the world.

James E. Hewes has written:

> President Roosevelt at the outset of World War II chose to exercise his role as commander-in-chief actively by dealing directly with General Marshall on strategy and military operations, bypassing the secretary of war. As a result, General Marshall in reality did command the army throughout the war under the president's direction.[1]

On the navy side, Executive Order 9096, dated 12 March 1946, made King the unchallenged head of the navy:

> As commander-in-chief, United States fleet, the officer holding the combined officers (chief of naval operations) as herein provided shall have supreme command of the operating forces comprising the several fleets, seagoing forces, and sea frontier forces of the United States Navy and shall be directly responsible, under the general direction of the secretary of the navy, to the president.[2]

Regarding who controlled the military strategy and operations of the war, President Roosevelt gave the Joint Chiefs a great deal of freedom. Army General George C. Marshall was the key figure on the army side. The army was the controlling agent for the war in Europe and General Marshall was the person responsible for everything from military strategy and administration to training and logistics, and to a lesser degree, by his own choosing, operations. He still was the key figure of the U. S. victory in Europe. All field commanders either directly or indirectly reported to him. These included Generals Eisenhower, Bradley, MacArthur, and Patton, and no one doubted who was the boss.

Regarding the Pacific war, the key figure was five-star Fleet Admiral Ernest J. King. Like General Marshall in Europe, he was the driving force of the U. S. victory over Japan. In fact, because he was not only chief of naval operations but also commander-in-chief of the United States fleet, Admiral King had, outside of his JCS responsibilities, direct control over the fleet. The basic strategy used by Admiral King was the Orange Plan, which was developed in 1907 and had been updated at the Naval War College by officers like Admirals King, Nimitz, and Spruance. All the major naval leaders of the war—Nimitz, Halsey, and Spruance—reported to Admiral King.

Fleet Admiral Chester Nimitz was the commander-in-chief of the Central Pacific Ocean area and the man responsible for carrying out the strategy that came from the Joint Chiefs of Staff in Washington. Because Admiral King had the active titles of commander-in-chief of the U. S. fleet and chief of naval operations, he was the unquestioned head of the navy and Marine Corps. Admiral Nimitz was responsible for clearing all important strategic, tactical, and personnel decisions with Admiral King, particularly when it involved the fleet.

Contrary to what many people believe, President Roosevelt basically stayed out of how the military carried out the political/strategic decisions he had made. He trusted and respected Admiral King and General Marshall and he let them essentially run the purely military part of the war. President Roosevelt only stepped in when there was conflict or when he felt a military decision was really more political or strategic. An example of this would be the invasion of North Africa in 1942, Operation "Torch," which was opposed by Admiral King and General Marshall but favored by the British and, ultimately, approved by President Roosevelt.

A similar situation happened in the Pacific where President Roosevelt supported Admiral King and, against the advice of people like General MacArthur, ordered the navy to take Guadalcanal. According to Admiral Morison, this ended up being one of the key decisions of the Pacific war. Morison put it this way:

> Nevertheless, King felt it necessary to stop the enemy's southward advance without delay . . . to MacArthur he wrote the same day (10 July) that he could not sanction any delay. Even if additional demands for Operation "Torch" or elsewhere should postpone the follow-up into the Solomons, the Tulagi operation must go on.
>
> He was right . . . this new Japanese spearhead had to be cut off then and there, lest it sever the lifeline between the United States and "Down Under." In accepting the grave responsibility for ordering the seizure of these islands, Admiral King made one of the great decisions of the war.[3]

The point is if one military man was running the show, we might have lost the flexibility that the Joint Chiefs of Staff gave us. The Germany-first concept was correct, but not if it was to the total exclusion of the Pacific war. As Lawrence Korb has written:

> Moreover, the war in the Pacific was shortened primarily because the Navy had been free to keep insisting within the JCS that a limited offensive in the Pacific would not interfere with victory in Europe. Under the single chief-of-staff system the CNO would not have such opportunity.[4]

Robert Sherwood, in his book, *Roosevelt and Hopkins,* made the point quite clearly regarding President Roosevelt's not getting overly involved in how the Joint Chiefs ran the war. Mr. Sherwood put it this way:

> For Roosevelt respected the judgment of his Chiefs of Staff, and there were not more than two occasions in the entire war when he overruled them.[5]

In his book on the Normandy Invasion, Gordon A. Harrison makes the point that President Roosevelt generally was an advocate of what the chiefs wanted to do. Harrison wrote:

He tended to make only the large decisions as between fully developed alternative courses of action . . . the president generally appeared at the Allied conferences as the defender of the strategy worked out by the Joint Chiefs of Staff.[6]

Fleet Admiral William D. Leahy, who was the president's personal chief-of-staff and a member of the Joint Chiefs, disagreed with Robert Sherwood and Gordon Harrison. It was his opinion that Roosevelt ran the war. He wrote:

Planning of major campaigns was always done in close cooperation with the president. Frequently we (the Joint Chiefs) had sessions in his study. And again Churchill and Roosevelt really ran the war.[7]

Kent Roberts Greenfield believed strongly that Roosevelt was both the key civilian and military leader of the war and that he controlled everything that went on. Mr. Greenfield wrote:

This resolves itself into the use he made of his authority, under the Constitution, as commander-in-chief of the armed forces. This authority of the American president is undefined and it has never been possible to distinguish it sharply from his other powers. But the theme of the present chapter can be exactly defined. It is Mr. Roosevelt's exercise of that power in decisions that, whatever their motivation, had a marked effect in determining to what uses the military resources of the nation were put.[8]

I believe Mr. Greenfield and Admiral Leahy were absolutely right when it came to grand strategy but much less so when it came to military operations, logistics, and personnel. For example, both Admiral King and General Marshall put the officers they wanted into top command and made extremely important decisions without getting President Roosevelt's specific approval.

In modern warfare, it is extremely difficult to make a clear distinction between what is a pure political decision versus one which is purely military. Surely, President Roosevelt understood that he was responsible for what ultimately happened and he would step in whenever he thought it necessary. But, just as important, he stayed away from those military areas that were being well managed. He knew he could not be a sideline player like President Wilson was in World War I. He also knew that he could not make all decisions. That was his genius.

James E. Hewes, Jr., wrote:

> President Franklin D. Roosevelt's decision to exercise an independent role in determining political and military strategy was more consistent with the traditional concept of the president as commander-in-chief developed by George Washington, James Madison, James K. Polk, Abraham Lincoln, and William McKinley. Even if Roosevelt had not deliberately chosen to play an active role, the vital political issues raised by World War II would have forced him to do so. Every major decision on military strategy was almost always a political decision as well and vice versa. There was, consequently, no clear distinction between political and military considerations during World War II.[9]

The following two decisions made by President Roosevelt give clear insight into his philosophy of decision making during the war. The first involved a decision about command between Admiral Nimitz and General MacArthur. Here is how E. B. Potter, biographer of Admirals Nimitz and Halsey, described it:

> MacArthur insisted that the question of who was in command be submitted to the president on 11 March. Admirals Leahy, King, and Nimitz brought the matter up in a White House discussion on Pacific strategy. Somewhat impatiently, Mr. Roosevelt replied that he didn't know

exactly where Manus was, and anyway the command problem was something the Joint Chiefs should handle.[10]

Another instance involves the decision to invade the Philippines instead of Formosa. Contrary to what most people believe, President Roosevelt did not make the final decision at his famous Pearl Harbor meeting with Nimitz and MacArthur. Again, E. B. Potter:

> That evening, in a conference with only the president, MacArthur, Nimitz, and Leahy present, the general pointed out that thousands of Filipino guerrillas were already harassing the Japanese occupation forces, that nearly the entire Filipino population could be counted on to join an American campaign of liberation . . . the president found these arguments convincing but did not impose his opinion on the Joint Chiefs.[11]

During World War II, President Roosevelt had Admiral King and General Marshall reporting directly to him for how the war would be run. The roles of the secretaries of war and navy were somewhat downgraded when it came to purely military matters.

In Richard F. Haynes's book, *The Awesome Power,* Harry S. Truman, as commander-in-chief, wrote:

> Roosevelt's direct command of the military during World War II was effected by his issuance of a formal military order in July 1939. The order removed from the service departments the Joint Army-Navy Board and a number of procurement agencies and placed them in the executive office of the president. Among other things this order had the effect of placing the chief of naval operations and the chief of staff of the army directly under the command and supervision of the commander-in-chief.[12]

President Roosevelt made absolutely sure that he was always in a position to control events by having the power to say yes or no even on operations. But in the final analysis—even though he clearly had the power to do otherwise—he did trust Admiral King and General Marshall and he did let them, to an extraordinary degree, run the war. Wilbur Morrison wrote:

> During subsequent meetings to determine basic policy, President Roosevelt frequently glanced at King when a suggestion was made by Churchill or other members of the British delegation. If King shook his head slightly, Roosevelt would emphatically turn down the suggestion, even if it came from Churchill. The Combined Chiefs of Staff determined the course of the war from then on.[13]

The more I think about Roosevelt as a manager and selector of men for leadership positions, the more respect I have for him. He chose Henry L. Stimson, Frank Knox, Averell Harriman, Dwight D. Eisenhower, Omar N. Bradley, Chester W. Nimitz, Raymond A. Spruance, John J. McCoy, Robert P. Patterson, James V. Forrestal, Robert A. Lovett, and of course, the magnificent General of the Army George C. Marshall and superb Fleet Admiral Ernest J. King.

As General Lord Ismay, Churchill's chief of staff, wrote:

> The Joint Chiefs of Staff remained together until the end of the war, except for the addition of Admiral Leahy as chairman in December 1942. When one recalls the number of changes which Lincoln had to make before he found General Grant, President Roosevelt must be accounted fortunate in his original choice of military advisers.[14]

I don't happen to think Roosevelt was as lucky as he was shrewd. I believe he knew a good man when he saw one and he also knew how to use them. The key to President Roosevelt as an effective leader was his ability to define objectives and to have information flowing into him from many sources. This is how he knew when to step in and when to leave well enough alone.

Roosevelt had to manage a world war on two fronts but he

did not have to be concerned with somebody in the field placing him in a position where use of the atomic bomb had to be considered. This fact gave him the time needed to consider the alternatives of grand strategy. The discovery of the atomic bomb would begin to further blur the distinction and importance between political, strategic, and military operations while greatly intensifying the political importance of military decisions.

CHAPTER III

KOREA

Harry S. Truman and the Need to Fire MacArthur

BECAUSE OF THE ATOMIC BOMB, I DON'T BELIEVE any American president will ever allow as much freedom to his military commanders as did President Roosevelt. Contrary to what is generally understood, President Truman kept much greater control of the military than did President Roosevelt. I would attribute this major change to the reality of the atomic bomb, which made it much easier for the military to take action on the battlefield that could have devastating consequences for the country. Here is how Richard F. Haynes put it in *The Awesome Power:*

> The Joint Chiefs and the service secretaries found that they, too, were dealing with a very different leader. Al-

> though Truman did have to be brought up to date on current operations, he was not dependent upon the military for command decisions. In fact, the new commander-in-chief "acted as a full-fledged master of the guild from the day he took office." It was Truman's conviction that the president must be the absolute commander of the country's armed forces. He believed he should set guidelines for the military, approve their strategy and major tactical recommendations when proper, and see to it that they implemented the policies of the administration. The most obvious immediate change that Truman made with respect to the command function was that, unlike Roosevelt, he insisted that all military decisions above the very routine receive his approval prior to their implementation. He has given his reasons for this: "I took the position that the president, as the commander-in-chief, had to know everything that was going on. I had had just enough experience to know that if you are not careful the military will hedge you in."[1]

Korea was the first war in our history to include the existence of the atomic bomb from beginning to end. Korea was a limited war but the reality of atomic power was ever present. At a press conference during the war, Truman was asked about our possible use of the bomb. He implied that its use was always under consideration.[2]

Because the Korean War was the first war that started with the potential use of atomic weaponry, President Truman had a unique responsibility. Robert Donovan said:

> For nearly eight years Truman was the president who had to manage the American adjustment to the changed world. He was the first president who had to decide whether to use the atomic bomb and how to compete with the Soviet Union in the development of nuclear and thermonuclear weapons. It was his decision in 1950 to build the hydrogen bomb. . . . It was Truman's policies that established the framework in which all the postwar presidents, including Johnson, shaped their own policies.[3]

On June 25, 1950, North Korea attacked South Korea and the United States was faced with a situation it never thought could happen again—a conventional war. To say the least, our conventional military capability was dangerously limited.

Clay Blair in his book, *The Forgotten War,* wrote:

> By June 25, 1950, Harry Truman and Louis Johnson had all but wrecked the conventional forces of the United States. The fault was Truman's alone . . . he had allowed his obsessive fiscal conservatism to dominate his military thinking and decisions.[4]

Think of this—the Pentagon budget was a dreadfully low $12.1 billion.

Everything from the number of divisions we had to how well they were trained was totally inadequate. Only five years after World War II had ended the American military was conventionally weak and, most important, had no strategy for using the atomic bomb. The army did not begin to seriously think about strategy in the nuclear age until after 1950.

In *Korea: The Untold Story of the War,* Joseph C. Goulden said:

> Truman and Acheson put the United States into a war that the American military was unprepared to fight and in fact had been told it would not have to fight.[5]

The reality was that the United States was going to war completely unprepared in every way. In his book, *Policy and Direction: The First Year,* James F. Schnabel outlined the deplorable position we were in:

> The Far East Command had received no new vehicles, tanks, or other equipment since World War II. Almost 90 percent of the armament equipment and 75 percent of the automotive equipment in the hands of the four combat divisions on that date was derived from the rebuilt program . . . on the eve of the storm the command was flabby and soft, still hampered by an infectious lassitude, un-

> ready to respond swiftly and decisively to a full-scale military emergency.[6]

General Ridgway, the genuine hero of the Korean War, put it even more forcefully:

> We were, in short, in a state of shameful unreadiness when the Korean War broke out, and there was absolutely no excuse for it. The only reason a combat unit exists at all is to be ready to fight in case of sudden emergency, and no human being can predict when these emergencies will arise. The state of our army in Japan at the outbreak of the Korean War was inexcusable.[7]

With our troops unprepared to fight and without a clear political policy, the delicate relationship between General MacArthur, as theatre commander, and President Truman would be severely tested. This would be a real test between the civilian authority of the president versus the tradition of giving the field commander a great deal of autonomy.

This test of authority started almost immediately by decisions made by General MacArthur without having proper approval from his superiors in Washington. Schnabel wrote:

> Before the day was out, General MacArthur ordered General Walker to load the MSTS Keathley, then in Yokohama Harbor . . . these actions MacArthur took independently. He received no authority from the JCS to supply the ROK until the following day, at 1330, 26 June.[8]

The big decision of whether to put American troops into Korea had to be made and President Truman clearly made it. Schnabel wrote:

> Throughout this period of intensive search for decisions culminating finally in the decision to meet the aggressor in ground combat, the president of the United States had been the ultimate arbiter of each step. President Truman

had solicited the advice of those best qualified to judge the military effects and requirements of each move taken. General Collins briefed him daily, passing on the views of the Joint Chiefs. But the president made the final choice himself.[9]

Because of our low state of readiness and worldwide responsibilities, the Joint Chiefs did not favor our using ground troops in Korea. So President Truman was making a delicate decision that placed him between the Joint Chiefs and General MacArthur, his field commander.

Secretary of Defense Louis A. Johnson also opposed using American ground troops in Korea. He also was for keeping very tight controls on General MacArthur. In *Korea: The Untold Story of the War,* Joseph C. Goulden wrote:

> Johnson advocated keeping a tight rein on MacArthur; his instructions "should be detailed so as not to give him too much discretion." No presidential authority should be delegated to MacArthur. Johnson, too, opposed putting ground troops into Korea.[10]

Despite President Truman's involvement in the military and his desire to control political/strategic policy, MacArthur continued his policy of trying to do what he wanted, even if this was not necessarily what Washington wanted. For example, regarding the bombing of bases in North Korea, he clearly did as he thought best—not what the Joint Chiefs of Staff directed. Goulden wrote:

> The JCS, although they had not *authorized* MacArthur to bomb beyond the 38th Parallel, had not *forbidden* him to do so either. A field commander should be permitted his normal discretionary powers in a battle situation. If North Korea remained a sanctuary, the Communists could continue to mobilize and supply forces south of the 38th Parallel . . . the more MacArthur talked—to himself and to sympathetic listeners—the firmer he felt the

> ground of traditional military practice beneath him. At 8 A.M. he dictated a message: "Partridge from Stratemeyer. Take out North Korean airfields immediately. No publicity. MacArthur approves. . . ." The episode also shows MacArthur at his worst, as a commander willing to perform intellectual gymnastics to evade doing as he was told.[11]

Right from the start General MacArthur was thinking about taking on the Chinese. He thought this was the right policy and he was going to find a way to use the Korean War as a means of getting at the Chinese. When asked a question by General Vandenberg, the air force chief-of-staff, about the Chinese getting into the war, General MacArthur answered:

> I would cut them off in North Korea. . . . In Korea I would visualize a cul-de-sac. The only passages leading from Manchuria and Vladivostok have many tunnels and bridges. I see here a unique use for the atomic bomb to strike a blow which would require a six months' repair job.[12]

From the initial period of defeat resulting in the Pusan perimeter and then our breakout at Inchon, the war went extremely well for the United States and particularly for Douglas MacArthur. But the time of testing was coming quickly as the U. N. forces passed the 38th Parallel and moved towards the Manchurian border and what turned out to be a totally new war involving the Red Chinese.

The whole issue of civilian control of the military was extremely important to President Harry S. Truman particularly because of his concerns about the atomic bomb and our lack of worldwide military preparedness. President Truman knew every effort had to be made to limit the war to Korea. It is clear, in retrospect, that had he known our move into North Korea would have provoked the Chinese or the Russians, then he surely would not have gone beyond the 38th Parallel. (In later years this decision would have great importance in the strategy we used in Vietnam.) MacArthur's success at Inchon had, unfortunately, paralyzed the Joint Chiefs so President Truman was not informed or forced to think through what our going beyond the 38th Parallel could mean. The fact is it could have meant the introduction of atomic weapons into Korea. General Ridgway wrote:

> There was also the possibility that the Russians, if they chose to enter the war, might do it by dropping an atomic bomb on Pusan and Inchon, the Korean harbors through which five-sixths of our supplies were flowing.[13]

Considering the consequences of a mistake, I find it surprising that Harry Truman did not foresee the problems he would have with MacArthur. The general was a strong person with very distinct views, and he had been in the Far East for a long time. In my opinion the president should have made his views quite clear to the general, precisely what he wanted accomplished, and very early in the process. Why he didn't do it probably had something to do with MacArthur's larger-than-life reputation.

President Truman erred in not making his political objectives clear to General MacArthur and in how he expected his field commander to carry out directions, particularly at the Wake Island conference. For any American president to leave an issue of this importance open-ended is a mistake. This became a costly one in Korea. After he was forced to fire General MacArthur, President Truman wrote:

> (MacArthur) understood military procedure and he also knows better than to try to run the policy of the United States Government from the Far East. If he didn't know better before he knows now.[14]

Any president would do better to tell his field commander what he expects done and precisely what the consequences would be for challenging presidential authority.

General MacArthur had little respect for, as he liked to say, the haberdasher from Missouri. He thought the fact that

Truman was president of the United States was just a minor reality that he would deal with by using his extreme popularity and the fact that he had the power, as field commander, to make the decision that he wanted executed in Korea.

General MacArthur also had little real respect for the Joint Chiefs of Staff, whom he thought of as bureaucrats who did not have the guts to act. To a large extent he turned out to be right. On many occasions the other chiefs, like General Collins, Admiral Sherman, and General Vandenberg, could have acted but continually chose to support the field commander. This same logic, unfortunately, applied to General of the Army and Chairman of the Joint Chiefs Omar N. Bradley, who did not deal firmly with General MacArthur on any critical issue that I know of.

With people like General Bradley, it never was a question of who was right or wrong. He knew the president was right but he didn't understand when the field commander must be told what to do. Somehow the men in Washington thought there was something wrong with giving the field commander an order. General Bradley said:

> That night I thought long and hard. Truman, as president and commander-in-chief, had established our policy for the conduct of the Korean War. MacArthur was clearly opposed to that policy and had openly and defiantly challenged it to the point where there was a serious question that he would carry out that policy.[15]

As a five-star general and as chairman of the Joint Chiefs, surely General Bradley could have done more to prevent President Truman from getting into a position where the commander in the field actually might not carry out orders from the president of the United States. General Bradley should have gone to Korea and told General MacArthur who was running our policy and the war. The facts are the men in Washington were, and continue to be, confused regarding the direct relationship between political policy, strategy formation and tactical effectiveness. No field commander must ever even think about functioning on his own. Political policy must always be the key factor driving events. That's why we have an active commander-in-chief.

Because the chiefs did not act, we ended up in Korea in a position of either risking a nuclear war or having our democratic system of government threatened. Joseph Goulden wrote:

> Bradley summarized the JCS thinking. . . . All members of the JCS have expressed from time to time their firm belief that the military must always be controlled by civil authorities. They were all concerned in this case, that if MacArthur was not relieved, a large segment of our people would charge that civil authorities no longer controlled the military.[16]

Dean Acheson, our secretary of state at the time, put his views even more powerfully:

> . . . because a man with great popular support in the country, with great military reputation, great authority in the Congress, was defying the authority of the president of the United States himself. And this seemed to me to go to the very root of democratic government; it was threatening the control over the military by the president and the whole civil side of the government. It seemed to me that we were in the presence of the gravest constitutional crisis that perhaps the U. S. had ever faced and I say that quite seriously and not in any oratorical sense. I think it is quite as serious as any of the crises which were faced during the Reconstruction period after the Civil War, and might have completely overthrown the constitutional system.[17]

What the Goldwater-Nichols Act does, by making the JCS chairman so dominant, is make it much more difficult for civilian authority to act and to act *before* any major problems occur. Yes, a strong JCS chairman who is carrying out the president's orders is fine—but nobody can guarantee that this will always be the case. Military dominance, once created, can be difficult, if not impossible, to stop. President Truman's need to fire General MacArthur should have taught us this lesson.

Robert Donovan summarized the crisis situation we could have faced:

> It [firing MacArthur] did not crush Truman. A very important reason why it did not was that throughout, especially in the forthcoming Senate hearings on the relief of MacArthur, George Marshall, Omar Bradley, Lawton Collins, Forrest Sherman, and Hoyt Vandenberg stood solidly and unshakeably behind the president for all to see. If, on the contrary, the esteemed secretary of defense and the chairman and members of the Joint Chiefs of Staff had supported General MacArthur, Truman would have had a staggering task getting through his term.[18]

These words contain a powerful warning. Consider what could have happened had our military leaders not supported the president. Civilian authority must never be placed in a position where, to prevent a constitutional crisis, it needs the support of our military leaders. The Goldwater-Nichols Act takes the first large step in this direction.

The chiefs, in my view, also failed President Truman by not using the power and prestige of General of the Army George C. Marshall who was the secretary of defense. President Truman had put General Marshall into the job because he had the highest regard for him. This included not only respect for his integrity, which was beyond question, but also Truman's respect for General Marshall as a proven military leader with judgment and courage. In addition, as many people forget, General Marshall was MacArthur's boss during World War II. Unfortunately for the country and for President Truman, General Marshall never became a positive force in dealing with MacArthur and for making him follow administration policy and military direction from Washington whether MacArthur agreed or not.

General Marshall, unfortunately, believed the chiefs had to

act before he took any forceful action. He did not understand that, unlike World War II when he was Army Chief of Staff and superior to the secretary of war on purely military matters, the secretary of defense was now the sole military boss reporting to the president.

The facts are it was not the chiefs or Secretary Marshall who were the people responsible for proposing that General MacArthur be fired. They did eventually agree with the president, but unfortunately, the president had to initially decide on his own to fire MacArthur without advice from the chiefs. General Bradley said: "In the end the JCS agreed unanimously that MacArthur should be relieved."[19]

There is no question in my mind that General MacArthur had no understanding of or respect for civilian control of the military. As President Truman knew so well, any kind of irresponsible behavior by a field commander, particularly in the atomic age, could have easily led to a third world war.

President Truman, as would be expected, relied on men like Secretary of State Dean Acheson and Secretary of Defense George C. Marshall and the Joint Chiefs of Staff. However, they never really understood, until late in the process, that civilian control could not be paralyzed by the prerogatives of a field commander. For the chiefs to stay in the background had drastic consequences for the country. Had the chiefs, and particularly General Marshall, acted early and firmly, then President Truman might not have had to fire MacArthur or face the crisis that resulted from the Chinese entry into the war.

Richard E. Neustadt and Ernest R. May wrote:

> Marshall, then named secretary of defense, adhered to the traditional principle of noninterference with the field commander, the more so since the latter had an old suspicion of him, and accordingly did little to restrain MacArthur's reckless march toward the Chinese border.[20]

Secretary of State Dean Acheson summarized the whole situation:

> We had the clearest idea among ourselves of the utter madness and folly of what MacArthur was doing up North. We sat around like paralyzed rabbits while MacArthur carried out this nightmare . . . not one of us, myself prominently included, served [the president] as he was entitled to be served.[21]

General MacArthur believed that once the war started it was up to the field commander to make every decision. In the Senate hearings held after he was fired, he said:

> The general definition which for many decades has been accepted was that war was the ultimate process of politics; that when all other political means failed, you then go to force; and that when you do that, the balance of control . . . the minute you reach the killing stage, is the control of the military. A theater commander, in any campaign, is not merely limited to a handling of his troops; he commands that whole area politically, economically and militarily. You have got to trust at the stage of the game when politics fail, and the military takes over, you must trust the military.[22]

What General MacArthur had forgotten was the control kept on his activities during World War II, particularly by Fleet Admiral Ernest J. King, as the key figure on the Joint Chiefs for the Pacific. Interestingly enough, MacArthur's direct superior during all of World War II was General Marshall. Since World War II the Army Chief of Staff has not been superior to any field commander. The Goldwater-Nichols Legislation has just made this situation worse.

When President Truman fired General MacArthur, the difference in fundamental viewpoint between the two men was absolutely clear. Here is what President Truman said:

> It is fundamental . . . that military commanders must be governed by our laws and Constitution. In times of crisis, this consideration is particularly compelling.[23]

General MacArthur thought it would be good to defeat the Chinese while, in his view, we had the chance in Korea. The president, on the other hand, was worrying about what it would mean if indeed we had to fight China and possibly the Soviet Union—particularly considering the fact that the Russians also had the atomic bomb.

MacArthur thought that use of the atomic bomb against the Chinese was a good idea, just a natural extension of the evolution of new military equipment. President Truman, and particularly our allies, began to recognize the atomic bomb as something whose use had a meaning far beyond anything we could imagine. President Truman's goal was to make sure no circumstance arrived whereby we were forced to use the atomic bomb. General MacArthur never saw it this way. He was using his position as theatre commander to establish overall political/strategic policy. Unfortunately, he did not understand that in our system of government, this must be solely the responsibility of the president of the United States. In fact, policy and the presidency must be synonymous. MacArthur thought the issue was him versus Truman.

President Truman might very well have considered what James Reston had to say in an article right after General MacArthur was appointed as United Nations forces commander:

> Diplomacy and a vast concern for the opinions and sensitivities of others are the political qualities essential to this new assignment, and these are precisely the qualities General MacArthur has been accused of lacking in the past.[24]

MacArthur's ideas and attitude were clearly shown in issues like what troops would be used to get the United Nations' forces to the Yalu River. The Joint Chiefs had made it clear that they wanted only South Korean troops to approach the border. At an October 28, 1950 press conference, President Truman said:

> It was my understanding that only South Koreans would approach the northern frontier of their country. MacArthur quickly squashed this notion: "The mission of the United Nations forces," declared Tokyo, "is to clear Korea."[25]

On his own and in direct violation of his orders, General MacArthur ordered his commanders to "use any and all ground forces to secure all of North Korea."[26] Nothing could have been more brazen and irresponsible than this act by General MacArthur. The lesson is a clear one: A field commander must always have, in addition to a civilian boss in Washington, a military one as well.

D. Clayton James summarized:

> As brazen as was his reply, the Joint Chiefs again decided, astonishingly, to let his judgment stand. The principle of trusting the field or theatre commander was deeply in all four of them.[27]

Unfortunately, it took a long time, but eventually even General Collins, the army chief of staff, began to understand what General MacArthur's philosophy, as field commander, could mean to the country.

John W. Spanier wrote:

> "Moreover," Collins continued, "I don't agree and did not agree with General MacArthur's reply that it would not be possible to stop upon the high ground overlooking the Yalu . . . and they became concerned lest MacArthur again disobey the policy prescribed for him and thereby precipitate a military incident which might ignite a world war."[28]

Certainly in his decision to fire General MacArthur, President Truman had to consider the fact that the general decided to attack toward the Yalu even when it began to be clear—contrary to what he told Truman at the Wake Island conference—that the Chinese were indeed in North Korea and in large numbers. So, in a way, you could say it was MacArthur who determined the political policy that provoked the Chinese by attacking and trying to occupy all of North Korea, and contrary to orders, with American troops reaching the Yalu River. MacArthur not only wanted to defeat North Korea, he wanted to change the whole strategic balance in Asia by defeating China on the battlefields.

Our political leaders abdicated their political responsibility to General MacArthur. I sincerely hope the Goldwater-Nichols Act has not created a situation where powerful military leaders like the JCS chairman and the CINCs will be regularly making political decisions. Once started, a momentum like this will be difficult to stop and can easily lead to a constitutional crisis as almost happened in Korea.

As dangerous as it may sound and as contrary to civilian control of the military, General MacArthur made a distinction between loyalty to the country and loyalty to his civilian leaders. Amazingly, he said:

> I find in existence a new and heretofore unknown and dangerous concept that the members of our armed forces owe primary allegiance or loyalty to those who temporarily exercise the authority of the executive branch of the government rather than to the country and its Constitution which they are sworn to defend. No proposition could be more dangerous.[29]

General MacArthur was right—nothing could be more dangerous than a general who believed what he did about the role of civilian leaders in our form of government. Considering the Goldwater-Nichols Act, we must remember a JCS chairman or a unified or specified commander who agrees with General MacArthur can easily rise again.

In contrast here is how General Bradley answered a question at the MacArthur firing hearings:

> Senator Bridges: "Where does the loyalty to your country come in?"
>
> General Bradley: "I am loyal to my country, but I am also loyal to the Constitution, and you have certain elected

officials under the Constitution, and I wouldn't profess that my judgment was better than the president of the United States or the administration."[30]

The problem with MacArthur was that he chose not to understand that the American people elect the person they want to be president knowing that he or she is the temporary representative of our democracy and the protector of the Constitution. The American system cannot work if the authority of the presidency is challenged on this critical point.

President Truman created problems for himself by not standing up to MacArthur earlier. For instance, when it came to bombing the Yalu bridges and the bombing of Sinuigu, President Truman let MacArthur have his way after Deputy Secretary of Defense Robert Lovett had ordered General MacArthur not to take action. Finally, somebody in Washington had the courage to act—and Truman foolishly countermanded the order and, by backing off, sent MacArthur the wrong, dangerous message.

This attitude on the part of the administration to give the theatre commander what he wanted instead of what Washington thought was right was just plain bad policy. The issue really has to do with the extent of power a field commander should have in a limited war, particularly when the atomic bomb is always present in the background. I don't think President Truman, Secretary Acheson, General Marshall, or the chiefs understood that the atomic bomb and modern communications had totally changed the way we had to fight wars and that, therefore, more than ever, a field commander had to be sensitive to political policy. It's important to note that, even during World War II, the field commanders were controlled on all major decisions by the Joint Chiefs of Staff. This was the method used by President Roosevelt for making sure our military operations were in harmony with his political goals.

General MacArthur often complained about political decisions that were being made in Washington. But there never was any question regarding the authority of President Roosevelt or the Joint Chiefs of Staff to make these decisions, and they did. The biggest decisions involved our overall military strategy for winning the war in the Pacific. Of course, it ended up being primarily a naval war with General MacArthur in command of the Southwest Pacific area only. General MacArthur, contrary to what most Americans believe, had nothing to do with such major operations as Tarawa, Guadalcanal, Kwajalein, Saipan, Iwo Jima, Guam, or Okinawa. Nor did General MacArthur have any involvement with the crucial carrier battles of the war such as Midway, Coral Sea, the Battle of the Philippine Sea, or the Battle of Leyte Gulf, which, if you think about it, were primarily responsible for our victory in the Pacific. The war in the Pacific was run from Washington by Admiral King, as chief of naval operations and commander-in-chief of the U. S. fleet; and by Admiral Nimitz, as the central Pacific commander reporting to Admiral King from the Pacific.

Korea was the first limited war we fought and the first war we did not clearly win. The only way we could have won was by limiting our goal to winning back South Korea and not crossing the 38th Parallel and invading North Korea. The war would have been won after the Inchon landing and our relatively easy move to the 38th Parallel. Had we stopped here, the Chinese would not have entered the war.

Our objective was to keep the war limited in Korea and this was somewhat influenced by the atomic bomb. President Truman was worried about its use and therefore ended up in conflict with his theatre commander. In my view the bomb forced civilian leadership to begin keeping closer control of what the field commander was allowed to do. Had there been a better understanding of the strategic change created by the atomic bomb, then maybe our civilian leaders might have acted sooner to make sure their policy decisions were completely understood and carried out by the field commander.

Surely, the president and the chiefs could have and should have kept General MacArthur under greater control. However, in the end the issue became one of civilian control, which is why the president had no alternative but to fire General MacArthur.

CHAPTER IV

ATOMIC BOMB

Dwight D. Eisenhower and Massive Retaliation

WHEN DWIGHT D. EISENHOWER TOOK OVER AS PRESIDENT, the bomb became the factor that forced the Chinese to finally decide to quit fighting. The Chinese, because of the brilliant leadership of General Matthew B. Ridgway, knew they could not win the war. They believed President Eisenhower would use the bomb—and this they did not want. James Coates and Michael Kilian wrote:

> It ended only after newly elected President Dwight Eisenhower quietly threatened to use tactical atomic weapons. He deployed atomic artillery in Korea, stockpiled nuclear shells in staging areas, and allowed Chinese military intelligence to discover the fact.[1]

The bomb was a major factor regarding civilian control with both President Truman and President Eisenhower. Truman reinforced civilian authority by firing MacArthur and making it clear that the war would be kept limited. President Eisenhower used civilian control of the military and the bomb to make it clear that civilian authority would and could ultimately dictate policy. In both cases, the meaning of civilian control of the military was intensified because of the atomic bomb.

In the case of Korea, we were in a period of transition from World War II, essentially without the atomic bomb, to the Korean War where the bomb was a reality. Henry Kissinger put it precisely when he wrote:

> We added the atomic bomb to our arsenal without integrating its implications into our thinking.[2]

I believe this is exactly what the Goldwater-Nichols Act has not done. It has not understood that in the modern age, more than ever, political leaders must determine strategy and, under certain conditions, military implementation as well. The Goldwater-Nichols Act has not integrated nuclear thinking into political thinking. The legislation is dangerous because it tries to solve political issues by making changes that are purely military.

Because of his military background, it would be logical to expect that when General of the Army Dwight D. Eisenhower became president he might loosen the concept of civilian control of the military. This did not happen.

In fact, under his administration, the power of the secretary of defense was greatly strengthened. The Defense Reorganization Acts of 1953 and 1958 made the secretary of defense the clear leader of our military establishment, both civilian and military. The secretary—the one man reporting to the president—now controls the entire military establishment, including the giving of orders to the various combatant commanders around the world.

Here is how the power of the secretary was described in the Department of Defense Documents on Establishment and Organization 1944–1978:

To repeat, subject to the president and certain express prohibitions against specifically described actions on the part of the secretary as contained in the National Security Act, as amended *the power and authority of the secretary is complete and supreme.*[3]

Since 1947 the role and power of the secretary of defense had been in a constant state of change. The need for the president to have a strong right-hand man became increasingly important because of the atomic bomb. Alain Enthoven and K. Wayne Smith summarized the situation:

Recognition of the need for a strong secretary of defense grew out of the lessons of combined land and sea and air operations in World War II and Korea . . . the strict controls on the use of force dictated by the risks of nuclear conflict.[4]

What President Eisenhower must have recognized when he became president was that the Pentagon had poorly served President Truman during the Korean War. One of the problems was clearly with the role of the secretary of defense. Secretary Johnson was in the job when the war started and, not being qualified or respected by the military, was replaced by General Marshall.

However, General Marshall did not see himself as the key figure in the process. He was still living with his experience of World War II where Secretary of War Henry L. Stimson did not and could not challenge his authority as the then army chief of staff. So, on the MacArthur issue, General Marshall waited for the chiefs to take the lead—he never fully understood his role as secretary of defense. Walter Isaacson and Evan Thomas wrote:

In the fall of 1950, Marshall bent over so far backward to be neutral that he fell down, and abnegated his responsibility.[5]

Clark Murdock reflected further on the problems the secretary of defense was having with this new position:

> The weakness of central control during this period is reflected by the fact that not only were the services duplicating weapons systems but that any resolution of service disputes by the secretary of defense was quickly evaded by the supposedly subordinate services.[6]

Initially, President Eisenhower selected Charles E. Wilson as secretary of defense. Wilson was not highly rated by anybody in government and this eventually included the president. President Eisenhower made his point when he said: "Damn it, how in hell did a man as shallow as Charles Wilson ever get to be head of General Motors?"[7] Eisenhower wanted the chiefs controlled and directed by Secretary Wilson but he could not do it. Stephen Ambrose wrote:

> But the real reason for Eisenhower's unhappiness with Wilson was the secretary's inability to control the chiefs. . . . In December, Eisenhower summoned Wilson and the chiefs to the oval office . . . "As Commander-in-Chief he is entitled to the loyal support of his subordinates of the official position he has adopted, and he expects to have that support."[8]

General Ridgway did not think much of either Secretary Louis A. Johnson or Charles E. Wilson.

> I well recall one session in the office of Mr. Wilson, when the reductions in the army budget were under discussion.
>
> "Why don't you reduce the strength of your combat division?" he asked me. "Pull them down to 85 percent. Why don't you inactivate certain units? Just keep them on a cadre basis."
>
> To my mind this would have been a repetition of that tragic policy of retrenchment followed by a former secretary, Mr. Louis Johnson, when during the Truman administration we so skeletonized our forces in the Far East that we were almost helpless when the crudely armed mass armies of North Korea stormed south across the

> parallel. As Mr. Wilson spoke I thought of the brave men who died in those early days in Korea.[9]

President Eisenhower ultimately replaced Secretary Wilson with Neil H. McElroy and McElroy with Thomas S. Gates, Jr., who was a strong and effective defense secretary. General Lyman L. Lemnitzer rated Secretary Gates the best secretary of defense he had known.

It is interesting that President Eisenhower, a military hero, ended up by letting military spending be decided not by military necessity but by the economic goal of trying to achieve a balanced budget. The sum total of Eisenhower's military experience ended up in his establishing as his military policy the inflexible notion of "massive retaliation." General Maxwell Taylor said: "Massive retaliation could offer our leaders only two choices, the initiation of general nuclear war or compromise and retreat."[10] Much more than in the Truman administration, the atomic bomb became the total answer to all our military challenges. However, neither Truman nor Eisenhower ever came to grips with the issue of conventional war.

Clark Murdock wrote:

> The doctrine of massive retaliation, which threatened the use of nuclear weapons for a wide range of contingencies, had its roots in the desire for a balanced budget.[11]

So what the military ended up with was a budget not based on military needs but instead on Eisenhower's definition of economics. Here is how President Eisenhower analyzed the situation:

> American strength is a combination of economic, moral and military force. If we demand too much in taxes in order to build planes and ships, we will tend to dry up the accumulations of capital that are necessary to provide jobs for the millions or more new workers that we must absorb each year. . . .

> Let us not forget that the armed services are to defend a "way of life" not merely land, property or lives. So what I try to make the chiefs realize is that they are men of sufficient stature, training and intelligence to think of this balance—the balance between minimum requirements in the costly implements of war and the health of our economy.[12]

Army Chief of Staff Maxwell Taylor had a different view:

> The fixed defense budget, by accentuating the interservice struggle for funds, has become the prime cause of the service rivalry which is undermining national confidence in our military program.[13]

President Eisenhower ended up, by design, with his military policy dominated by the atomic bomb. He thought the bomb could not be used and, therefore, would serve as a deterrent to war. Production of the atomic bomb was, of course, much cheaper than having a large conventional capability, which the president believed would not be needed. Robert Lackie wrote:

> The bomb was also attractive to its proponents because it was relatively cheap to manufacture in large quantities. The idea was to "substitute machines for men." American technology would offset the mass armies of Asia, it was maintained, once again, discounting the truth that had emerged from Korea—that the ruthlessly regimented masses of Asia could, by ingenuity and a brutally indifferent expenditure of life and labor, make mockery of Western gadgetry.[14]

President Eisenhower could live well with this technological strategy, but Army Chief of Staff Maxwell Taylor believed it was dangerous to eliminate the conventional option. General Taylor wrote:

> After two years of the Eisenhower Administration, the main elements of its national security policy were fairly

> clear. They included placing main reliance on nuclear weapons to deter or defeat Communist aggression of all varieties and avoiding involvement in limited wars such as that in Korea. . . . "To evaluate such doubts, particularly among the military skeptics, President Eisenhower approved in October 1953 a National Security Council paper which authorized the JCS to plan on using nuclear weapons, tactical as well as strategic, whenever their use was desirable from a military standpoint."[15]

Eisenhower ended up controlling the military not by directly running the Pentagon but by controlling the budget which was the prime factor behind the concept of massive retaliation. What he did was put in place a policy which was, in many ways, civilian control in reverse. The madness of the bomb was the deciding factor. Russell Weigley wrote:

> On Dec. 9 the Joint Chiefs presented to Secretary Wilson a proposal to implement NSC/62/2. They stated their assumptions that in the next few years there would be no significant change in the intensity of international rivalry or in the ratio of Soviet to American power, that American nuclear retaliatory capacity was the major deterrent to both general and limited war, and that henceforth nuclear weapons would be employed not only in general war but when they were militarily useful in limited war.[16]

In the Eisenhower Administration, civilian control of the military was really not an issue. The president had no problem in handling the chiefs—but what some of the chiefs thought had little meaning considering the firm policy of massive retaliation based on economics.

At one point in 1954, when Chairman of the Joint Chiefs of Staff Admiral Arthur W. Radford recommended we use the navy and air force in Indochina, Eisenhower turned him down. Anthony Leviero:

> President Eisenhower has applied the check reins to Admiral Radford's ideas on two known occasions. He re-

> jected a proposal for a blockade of Red China favored by Senator Taft and by Admiral Radford (before he became chairman of the Joint Chiefs).
>
> Also, the president's experience in land warfare induced him reluctantly to avoid intervention as he had desired in Indochina. Admiral Radford had advised intervention with airpower and naval forces but not ground forces. The president agreed with General Ridgway that intervention would require forces comparable to those used in Korea.[17]

President Eisenhower's overall views regarding the war in Indochina were quite clear and definitive. He simply believed the French could not win. In a letter to General Alfred Gruenther, he wrote:

> As you know, you [Al Gruenther] and I started more than three years ago trying to convince the French that they could not win the Indochina war and particularly could not get real American support in that region unless they would unequivocally pledge . . . independence to the Associated States upon the achievement of military victory. Along with this . . . this administration has been arguing that no Western power can go to Asia militarily, except as one of a concert of powers, which concert must include local Asiatic peoples.
>
> To contemplate anything else is to lay ourselves open to the charge of imperialism and colonialism or—at the very least—of objectionable paternalism. Even, therefore, if we could by some sudden stroke assure the saving of the Dienbienphu garrison, I think that under the conditions proposed by the French the free world would lose more than it would gain.[18]

The president went on to make a series of statements which certainly look good considering what happened in Vietnam. President Johnson and his advisers would have done well to read these remarks by President Eisenhower before they decided to get the United States involved in a land war of attrition in Indochina. President Eisenhower said:

> The jungles of Indochina, however, would have swallowed up division after division of United States troops. . . . Furthermore the presence of ever more numbers of white men in uniform probably would have aggravated rather than assuaged Asiatic resentments. Thus, even had all of Indochina been physically occupied by United States troops, their eventual removal would have resulted only in a reversion to the situation which had existed before.[19]
>
> Any nation that intervenes in a civil war can scarcely expect to win unless the side in whose favor it intervenes possesses a high morale based upon a war purpose or cause in which it believes.[20]
>
> We have got to find a line which other people will be prepared to defend. We cannot carry, unwanted or unasked, the entire burden.[21]

I believe President Eisenhower served the nation quite well in Indochina but not as well regarding overall military policy formation. His emphasis on the country's economic strength and the budget ended up making an atomic war a distinct possibility under certain circumstances. The military ended up split, with people like Admiral Radford agreeing strongly with the president's policy, while others, like Army Chief of Staff Matthew Ridgway and Maxwell Taylor, totally disagreeing with the whole idea of massive retaliation and the country's overall military direction. General Taylor wrote:

> It is hard to be sure just where the strategic issue stood by the close of the Eisenhower Administration. To the end, there was never a clear indication of priorities among the functions to be performed by the armed forces, no yardsticks of sufficiency to serve as standards for performance by functional forces, little guidance as to the resources to expect for the tasks assigned.[22]

The other surprise of former General of the Army and now President Dwight D. Eisenhower was his famous speech at the end of his administration about the "Military-Industrial Complex." President Eisenhower understood the incredible amount of power in our military establishment. He understood the need to keep it under control both on the economic/business/supplier side and by having civilian control of the military, especially because of the atomic bomb.

Maybe that is why his most important contribution as president was his strengthening of the powers of the secretary of defense. I believe President Eisenhower understood that in the atomic age it is critical to have an unchallenged civilian secretary running the Department of Defense and reporting to the president, not solely to keep the military under control but also to be the focal point for the establishment of military strategy based on the president's political policy.

The Goldwater-Nichols Act assumes that increasing the power of one man—the chairman of the Joint Chiefs of Staff—will somehow improve military effectiveness. The legislation quite clearly focuses on military matters. My contention is that the problem, as happened in Vietnam, was political and civilian. Strengthening the JCS chairman does nothing but threaten the civilian control of our military establishment, which was so important to President Eisenhower.

CHAPTER V

CUBAN MISSILE CRISIS

John F. Kennedy, A Superb Example of Civilian Control

WHEN JOHN F. KENNEDY BECAME PRESIDENT, he had two important military factors to consider, both of which were inherited from the Eisenhower administration. The first was massive retaliation; the second, our lack of adequate conventional strength. As Cuba would ultimately show, it was fortunate that he moved quickly to strengthen the country's conventional capability.

To prevent the Soviets from keeping those missiles in Cuba, President Kennedy had to act prudently but also forcefully.

This phrase from his famous October 22 speech makes clear the critical role civilian leadership has in the nuclear age. The president said:

> It shall be the policy of this nation to regard any nuclear missile launched from Cuba against any nation in the Western Hemisphere as an attack by the Soviet Union on the United States, requiring a full retaliatory response upon the Soviet Union.[1]

In the case of the Cuban Missile Crisis, the bomb was well integrated into both our military and civilian thinking. As a result, the bomb was very important in the overall thinking that went on during the crisis, but in the end, the conventional strength of the United States is what carried the day.

The Cuban Missile Crisis was, because of the great number of nuclear bombs available on both sides, a much more critical test of civilian control of the military than had ever before been the case. Surely President John F. Kennedy understood the drastic consequences should something go wrong. Like President Truman fighting a limited war in Korea, he was moving into a totally new situation with the Cuban Missile Crisis and clearly his behavior and need to control military affairs was greatly affected by the existence of nuclear power.

Writing in *Swords and Plowshares,* General Maxwell Taylor summarized President Kennedy's experience:

> Overall he was frankly amazed and, I think, somewhat sobered by the evidence he saw of the military power at his disposal and the military consequences of his decisions.[2]

President Kennedy tried to keep every option open until the last possible moment during those critical days of October 1962 in order to give Chairman Khrushchev enough time to act rationally. As Robert Kennedy wrote in his book, *Thirteen Days:*

The president believed from the start that the Soviet chairman was a rational, intelligent man who, if given sufficient time and shown determination, would alter his position.[3]

President Kennedy always had to keep in mind the fact that if something really went wrong and war broke out with the Soviet Union, then indeed it could mean the end not only for them but for us as well. Unlike the past, no mistakes could be made. Military strategy and political policy were synonymous.

In addition, he had to keep in mind that Soviet missiles in Cuba were not only a military threat to the United States but also a question of prestige and power. The establishment of a Soviet missile base in Cuba had dramatic foreign policy consequences for the United States.

Based on the Bay of Pigs fiasco, Chairman Khrushchev considered President Kennedy weak and indecisive. At their meeting in Vienna, Chairman Khrushchev tested his hypothesis by trying to push the young, inexperienced president around. The chairman was trying to find out if indeed Kennedy had the guts to defend the vital interests and prestige of the United States of America.

Charles Burton Marshall summarized the importance of prestige when it comes to a great power:

> Prestige is the faculty enabling a great power to avoid final, miserable choices between surrender and war. Prestige is the ingredient of authority in international affairs . . . the quality that demands being listened to is prestige—and a nation suffers loss of it at great peril.[4]

The peril, of course, is that a miscalculation could be made that would result in war. The best situation for a nation to be in is to have the military capability necessary to avoid war. In modern times the real objective of military power is to have it available for all to see but never to actually have to use it. That is why so many Americans don't understand why it is right to always have many more military ships, planes, and guns than will ever be used, and that a perfect policy results in the non-use of any of our military capability. Trouble for the United States begins when our enemies believe we fall below that magic line of having more military power than is needed. The other key ingredient is the willingness to use it in defense of our vital interests.

During the Cuban Missile Crisis, President Kennedy kept very tight control over the military. He tried to do everything possible not to have anything get out of his personal control. He was clearly the commander-in-chief, not only for overall political/strategic policy but also for military operations. For example, even the way in which a ship trying to break the quarantine would be attacked was carefully controlled.

Alexander L. George wrote:

> If a confrontation took place with a vessel refusing to cooperate with the interdiction procedures, the navy was to shoot at the rudders and propellers of the vessel in order to avoid loss of life or the sinking of the ship.[5]

President Kennedy also had communications set up so that he personally had to give the order to board or fire on any Soviet vessel. This might be the first case where total control of the military was executed by a chief executive. The facts were that the reality of the atomic bomb forced President Kennedy into the position of taking this drastic step of not only controlling but actually running the military in every sense of the word.

In his book *Essence of Decision,* Graham T. Allison wrote:

> Kennedy reached out beyond the normal span of presidential awareness and influence to watch as many details as possible, to recheck potential slip-ups.[6]

President Kennedy was determined not to have events get out of his control. He wanted the military to understand precisely what he was trying to accomplish and what he expected them to do. Graham T. Allison:

> For the navy, the issue was one of effective implementation of a military mission—without the meddling and interference of political leaders. For the president, the problem was to pace and manage events in such a way that the Soviet leaders would have time to see, think, and blink.[7]

Here is how President Kennedy checked out the issue with Admiral Anderson:

> "You are certain it can be done?" the president inquired.
> "Yes, Sir!" responded the Admiral.[8]

The president clearly understood that in the final analysis he had to make the decisions. The decisions regarding war and peace belonged to him alone—not to any other civilian or military man. He knew there was no backing away from this one, as happened during the Bay of Pigs, because he didn't understand the big picture. In the case of the Cuban Missile Crisis, he could get help from others but he alone had to define the big picture. He had to decide how to use the military power of the United States in order to prevent war. Elie Abel wrote:

> The president alone, as commander-in-chief, had the power to decide and did in fact give the orders. The president's was the controlling intelligence. He ran the operation, one official recalls, "like a lieutenant runs a platoon in combat. Bundy, Rusk, Stevensen, and the rest were there to advise him. He listened, then made his own decisions."[9]

After the Bay of Pigs, I believe President Kennedy learned the importance of asking the right questions. It was both his way of finding out what was going on and also his way of effectively communicating his policy.

President Kennedy was always concerned that some military mistake could end up dictating policy. He found it was one thing to have ordered the missiles out of Turkey and quite another issue to make sure the order was carried out. Implementation, he learned, was equally as important as the original policy decision.

The importance of implementation is what President Kennedy was worried about and why he established direct contact between the oval office and the U. S. ships ensuring the quarantine. Lawrence Korb, in *The Chiefs of Naval Operations,* wrote:

> Throughout the crisis, political leaders in the basement of the White House communicated with and gave direct orders to the ships stationed along the quarantine line.[10]

Possibly for the first time in American history, the military people on the spot actually received direct orders from their civilian leaders at the top of government. Surely this makes the point regarding the supremacy of political policy over any other factor, including the chain of command, and the assumption of superior knowledge by the commander on the scene. Graham T. Allison wrote:

> Thus, for the first time in U. S. military history, local commanders received repeated orders about the details of their military operations directly from political leaders—contrary to two sacred military doctrines. This circumvention of the chain of command and the accompanying countermand of the autonomy of local commanders created enormous pain and serious friction.[11]

On the point of presidential control, the Goldwater-Nichols Act has really done nothing. It did not consider the relationship not only between the president and the military, but between the president and the secretary of defense. For example, could it just be that the secretary of defense is becoming more and more the commander-in-chief?

Under our system of government, the president's role as commander-in-chief must be active and unquestioned as it was, for example, with President Roosevelt during World War II. Roosevelt rarely made pure military decisions, but nevertheless, still controlled events. This was the great genius of the man.

No role is more important to any president than how effectively he or she functions as commander-in-chief. President Kennedy did it poorly at the Bay of Pigs and well during the Cuban Missile Crisis. President Johnson did it very poorly and with tragic consequences in Vietnam. But to believe that the Goldwater-Nichols Act does anything to improve the chance of presidential effectiveness is a dangerous illusion.

President Kennedy also made decisions that were designed to send clear signals to Khrushchev. The signals were that he was a reasonable man but that he had the power to act and would do so. A good example of this was where President Kennedy chose the *Marucla* as the first ship to be boarded. Alexander L. George wrote:

> This vessel, the *Marucla,* was carefully selected by the president for this purpose. Since it was a Panamanian-owned, Lebanese-registered vessel under Soviet charter, it could be stopped without offering a direct affront to the Soviets. At the same time, by stopping and searching a vessel carrying Soviet cargo, the President would demonstrate to Khrushchev that he was going to enforce the quarantine fully.[12]

President Kennedy, as commander-in-chief and as civilian head of our government, controlled every major decision of the crisis. The political and military options considered were those of our civilian leaders. Only General Taylor was included in the deliberation of the executive committee of the National Security Council. However, the president did see and get the views of the other chiefs. Even how the quarantine would be run was completely controlled by our civilian leadership. This total control was a direct reflection of what the cost of a mistake would be. The need for political policy to determine implementation was clear. Everything President Kennedy decided to do was a piece of communication to Chairman Khrushchev. Elie Abel wrote:

> The object of the operation was not to shoot Russians but to communicate a political message from President Kennedy to Chairman Khrushchev.[13]

When compared to World War II or even Korea, the Cuban Missile Crisis, because of the atomic bomb, forced President Kennedy into a new role as president. President Truman had fired General MacArthur in Korea to support the concept of civilian control of the military. This action also made clear the president's right to control strategy.

The Cuban Missile Crisis went one step further by making President Kennedy not only the strategic but also the operational decision maker of our military establishment. The idea of a field commander running the show after the president had established political policy was clearly not appropriate. The relationship between political policy and military strategy formation was too close. There was no question about the president's ability to act and no better case of complete civilian control and direction of the military. The key factor that made this a necessity was the threat of nuclear war.

During the Cuban Missile Crisis, President Kennedy learned precisely what it meant to be president of the United States and the need to be an active commander-in-chief in the nuclear age. This was in direct contrast to the Bay of Pigs where he failed so badly because he let events get out of his control. He learned from the Bay of Pigs not to rely on experts, and he applied this experience to his decision making during the Cuban Missile Crisis. As president, only he was in the best position to judge. Others saw part of the picture, only he could see it all and be totally responsible for what happened. In the end, he had to trust and rely on himself alone. A commander-in-chief must know when to act and, just as important, when someone else can do it better.

As no American in our history, President Kennedy had to live with the reality that if he made a mistake, it could mean the end of the world. No person is prepared to handle this kind of awesome responsibility. The atomic bomb made him the military chief of our country, commander-in-chief in every sense of the word. Maxwell Taylor wrote:

> Once this decision was made and implementation began, the same considerations that made him cautious in picking his first option made him wish to control personally the key actions of his military forces. He had tried to do this in the Bay of Pigs episode and had failed miserably. This time, however, he was better served by an established communications and command structure which enabled him to move naval units about the Caribbean almost by hand. This personal intervention was offensive to many of my military associates who regarded it as unwarranted civilian interference, but I did not agree with the criticism. The quarantine was a political gambit in a deadly serious game, and the master player on our side had every reason to keep his hand on the pawns. It was a classic example of the use of military power for political purposes which, after all, is the prime justification for military power.[14]

The formula for success in the Cuban Missile Crisis was a president who controlled events by being both head of state and commander-in-chief of our military forces. President Kennedy established clear political goals. These were precisely communicated to the military who, he made sure, understood them. The president also made sure the dominant military force needed for success was available. Initially, nuclear power was the single most important factor. But once the issue became clearer, it was our conventional strength that forced the Soviets to back off.

As all presidents must do, President Kennedy dealt with the chiefs on his terms during the Cuban Missile Crisis. He let them know what he wanted to accomplish and asked them how best to get the job done.

President Kennedy focused on one key factor after the crisis was over: If he had to act on the first day, he would have been forced to bomb the missile sites in Cuba. If the Goldwater-Nichols Act had been operating in 1962, I believe, it would have been much more difficult for President Kennedy to have received as much overall advice as he did. *A strong JCS chairman with military forces totally under his control could have put great pressure on the president to do what he wanted.* All governmental decisions of this kind involve politics based on bureaucratic influence, knowledge, and power which, in this case, could have favored the JCS chairman at the expense of the president. What the Goldwater-Nichols Act does, which is so dangerous in situations like this, is move the military bureaucracy toward the JCS chairman at the expense of the president, the secretary of defense, and the country.

CHAPTER VI

VIETNAM

Civilians Fail to Establish Political Policy Integrated with Military Responsibility

THE CUBAN MISSILE CRISIS WAS A NEAR-PERFECT EXAMPLE of a president acting as head of the government and as commander-in-chief of the military. First, as civilian head of the government, President Kennedy established the political policy needed to achieve success. Second, as commander-in-chief, he made sure the military knew precisely what they were expected to do and how this matched with his political objectives. This precision was the formula for success. Vietnam was quite a different matter; to find out why is a difficult task. To do this, I am going to analyze the key political and military decisions made during the administrations of Presidents Kennedy and Johnson.

Vietnam was a classic example of what will happen when a president doesn't execute his primary responsibility of establishing an overall political policy that is clear, well-communicated throughout the U. S. bureaucracy, and achievable. As Admiral Moorer testified:

> I would hope that we would never get into a military confrontation that was fought the way Vietnam was, because here was a conflict wherein the personnel were never really sure of what the national objectives were . . . there was never a clear-cut statement of national objectives.[1]

Things got worse when President Johnson and the secretary of defense tried to compensate for not having a clear policy by becoming tactical military experts. They did this at the expense of their primary civilian leadership responsibilities. Civilian leaders must only become involved in military implementation when policy issues are directly involved, as was the case during the Cuban Missile Crisis, or when military implementation is failing. Therefore, civilian leadership must know when it is appropriate to get involved and for what purpose. The purpose must always relate back to overall political policy—not just to meddle in military affairs. Because when civilian leaders do this, it will be at the expense of political policy formation and overall strategic supervision.

Admiral Moorer testified strongly on this point:

> I am a great believer in civilian control. And I think that that is the way the Constitution reads, and those in uniform are strict constitutionalists. However, I think that the military should be told what to do, but not how to do it. In the Vietnam war we used to be told how many

> bombs to put on each wing of the airplanes and what kind of bombs to use by people who had never seen a bomb.
>
> But I don't know how you are going to solve that in a democracy, if you have an administration that is manned by people, such as Secretary McNamara and his staff, who was supported by the president.[2]

To make things worse, Secretary McNamara and President Johnson were responsible for evaluating the effectiveness of military implementation—and they did not do it. As I will outline later, search and destroy tactics went on and on without review by anybody in authority—not the president, the secretary of defense, or the Joint Chiefs of Staff.

As we unfortunately learned, once a president creates a vacuum by not having a political strategy for victory, the result is political and military chaos. This is precisely what happened in Vietnam, particularly after President Lyndon B. Johnson escalated and made it an "American war" in 1965.

Vietnam was a directionless attempt to fight a war our civilian leaders never made relevant to the American people. Why they never understood the critical role of the American people in our system of government is quite surprising. By doing what he did the way he did it, President Johnson made the foolish error of making Vietnam a "president's war," not a "people's war." I don't believe the president ever understood his primary responsibility was to establish a clear political strategy which, above all else, would have the solid backing of the American people. General Bruce Palmer wrote:

> Our government, itself lacking a clear understanding of what it means and what it takes to commit a nation to war, failed to persuade the public that it was necessary for us to fight in Vietnam.[3]

The most important point for the American people to keep in mind is that Vietnam was primarily a civilian disaster, not a military one. This does not mean the military was perfect—it does mean the responsibility for what went wrong belongs to our civilian leaders. As Dave Richard Palmer wrote, "The inability to foresee what form the war would take was the first great failure of our military involvement in Vietnam."[4] Unfortunately, none of our civilian leaders, particularly President Johnson and Secretary McNamara, ever understood how to fight a counterinsurgency war.

Sometimes people confuse what ultimately happened in Vietnam with who was responsible for the quality of the decisions being made. In the American system, the responsibility even for what happens on the battlefield must belong to our civilian leaders. I believe the Goldwater-Nichols Act, by making the chairman of the Joint Chiefs so powerful, takes our eye off civilian responsibility, including that of Congress. The point is, unlike what happened in Vietnam, political strategy must always dominate military strategy thus creating a political task that is achievable by the military. And this does not mean civilians make important military decisions without consulting or respecting military advice.

As it must be in our free democratic society, the decision to fight in Vietnam, and to the extent we did, was made by our civilian leaders in the executive branch; and they—the president, the secretary of state, the secretary of defense and the national security adviser—are primarily responsible for what resulted.

Former Defense Secretary Caspar W. Weinberger said:

> Policies formed without a clear understanding of what we hope to achieve would also earn us the scorn of our troops, who would have an understandable opposition to being *used*—in every sense of the word—casually and without intent to support them fully. Surely the lack of respect and gratitude we showed to our brave Vietnam veterans was one of the low points in U. S. history. It must never happen again.[5]

Fortunately, civilian control of the military was never an issue during the Vietnam war. The military establishment did what it was supposed to do: follow orders. The thought that it would have done anything else is chilling indeed. Many

Americans got confused with the objectives of the war and, therefore, believed the military had the right to disregard orders. Here is how former Army Chief of Staff Fred C. Weyand and Harry Summers, Jr., brilliantly challenged this logic:

> During the Vietnam war there were those—many with the best of intentions—who argued that the army should not obey its orders and should refuse to serve in Vietnam. But their argument that soldiers should obey the "dictates of their conscience" is a slippery slope indeed. At the bottom of this slope is military dictatorship.[6]

I believe the Goldwater-Nichols Department of Defense Reorganization Act of 1986 is, to some extent, a reaction to the failure of Vietnam. It does not include the civilian/military lessons learned since World War II, such as the need for civilians to dominate events by controlling political grand strategy not by becoming instant field commanders. This lack of historical perspective has made the bill narrow in focus and counterproductive. Most important, it contributes nothing towards improving the relationship and decision-making capability between the executive branch, the Congress, and the military.

Clearly the executive branch of the government was primarily responsible for what happened in Vietnam, but surely Congress cannot continue to escape all blame for its lack of involvement until the tragic defeat of the United States was obvious. Said another way, Congress made no positive contribution whatsoever to what happened in Vietnam. Admiral Moorer:

> I think Congress never did question the details of how this war was really being managed.[7]

I hope this will be the last time Congress will sit on the fence when America is at war. If we are to be successful in any future war, Congress and the executive branch must find new ways to work together to establish overall political strategy and get public support. As the final Packard Commission Report said:

> Today, there is no rational system whereby the executive branch and the Congress reach coherent and enduring agreement on national military strategy, the forces to carry it out and the funding that should be provided.[8]

Now it is simple and clear for Congress to make it seem like all the mistakes in Vietnam were military. Just make drastic changes in the military establishment, corresponding changes in the executive branch but, most interesting, no changes in what Congress does or will be held accountable for. Is this the lesson of that tragic war, and what needs to be done to prevent a Vietnam from happening again? Will throwing more power to the JCS chairman really improve decision making and the overall effectiveness of our military establishment?

If the Goldwater-Nichols Act is left unchanged, we run the risk of not learning the key lesson of the Vietnam war: never fight a war without a clear political policy that has the complete backing of the executive branch (the bureaucracy), Congress and, most important, the American people. The Goldwater-Nichols Act incorrectly implies that accomplishing this important objective has something to do with the chairman of the Joint Chiefs of Staff. It does not. If we have to fight again, it must be with the people's army. If not, we run the risk, as happened in Vietnam, of having it destructively defined as "Johnson's war" or "McNamara's war"—not the "people's war."

In a democracy the military must never be used except as an extension of the will of the people. The decision regarding whether we use military power and the need for getting the support of the people must be shared by the executive branch and Congress. The executive branch can no longer go it alone—Congress must become a more positive force. The need for finding a new way for the executive branch and Congress to work together is one of the prime lessons of Vietnam. The Goldwater-Nichols Act does not touch on this crucial issue.

Now let's change the focus a bit. Can you imagine what

could happen in a future war or other crisis situations where a powerful chairman of the Joint Chiefs uses his dominance of the chiefs and the CINCs to challenge civilian authority? That is a road which, once started, leads to the end of our democracy. Fortunately, this probably will not happen immediately because our system has been so fundamentally sound. As proof, we have the history of the last 200 years, but who knows about the future after the Goldwater-Nichols Act has been allowed to create a new, unknown direction? So not only does the Goldwater-Nichols Act not answer the problems of Vietnam, but it also creates two new problems:

- A possible challenge sometime in the future to civilian control of the military that would threaten our very democracy.
- Creation of a revised decision-making arrangement that allows the concept of joint operations to dominate all thinking at the expense of flexibility and individual service excellence. The facts are air, ground, and naval operations are monumental matters within themselves and not always best merged by considering joint operations first. Also, if the Goldwater-Nichols Act is right, then we should no longer have an army, an air force, a navy, and a Marine Corps. One service would be the answer—the wrong answer. Why? Because the spirit, history, and tradition of our separate services is one of the nation's greatest assets. Because even when we have to fight on a joint basis, the specific operations are best accomplished by experts in either ground, air, or naval warfare. The point of military coordination must be principally at the end of the process. You need an effective army, navy, Marine Corps, and air force on which to build successful joint military operations.

Vietnam was a Washington mistake. The executive branch failed to establish a sound political policy on which to win a war. The president and the secretary of defense meddled too much in military tactical detail. The double negative here is that neither President Johnson nor Secretary McNamara understood their critical role in supervising and evaluating strategic military plans. The Joint Chiefs failed in two ways. First, they let the war be run by the field commanders. Second, they never told their civilian leaders that the war was not winnable using the strategy they had selected. Congress failed because it did not get involved until it was too late to prevent so much of the tragedy.

* * *

The rest of this chapter considers the Goldwater-Nichols Act within the specific context of the Vietnam war. No attempt has been made to make this a history of that war. What I have done is focus on the issues of authority and responsibility for what ultimately happened in Vietnam. The key question we must ask ourselves is precisely how would the Goldwater-Nichols Act have helped political decision making and our war-fighting effectiveness?

The issues I focused on include:

- Trying to prove that we had no political strategy for winning the Vietnam war.
- Showing why the military in Vietnam ended up in a no-win position politically and militarily.
- Showing why the Goldwater-Nichols Act tries to replace the responsibility of the president and the secretary of defense with that of a strong chairman of the Joint Chiefs of Staff.
- Showing why the point of responsibility for military/political recommendations going to the president must stay with the secretary of defense, and why this advice must include the thinking of *all* the chiefs, not just the chairman.

Let us now focus on the point of whether or not we had a political strategy for winning the war defined as keeping South Vietnam from being taken over by North Vietnam.

We lost in Vietnam because we never had a strategy for winning. Considering the political problems in South Vietnam—their inability to govern themselves—the only way to have achieved total victory would have been for the United States to invade and occupy North Vietnam. Even if we could have achieved this goal militarily, consider what China and the Soviet Union might have done. The American people just would not have supported this strategy because it would have involved a long war whose strategic importance to the U.S. was unclear.

The Vietnam war can best be described as a political struggle beyond our capacity to control. It was very similar to what happened to the British during our War of Independence. The British could not control the country without being able to control the people—no matter how good they were militarily. Our involvement in Vietnam could and did give us a measure of control, but it never could be the *dominant* factor, particularly with the attrition strategy selected by the army. This fact was evident to President Kennedy but never ended up as the dominant factor in the ultimate strategy which was, unfortunately, decided by President Johnson.

Here is how President Kennedy saw it:

> Experience has taught us that no one nation has the power or the wisdom to solve all the problems of the world or manage its revolutionary tides; that extending our commitments does not always increase our security.[9]

President Kennedy understood the limitations of what could be achieved in Vietnam. The civil war and revolutionary complexities made what the United States could accomplish quite limited. As Lyndon Johnson would find out, brute force, used without a well-thought-out political strategy, against an enemy whose political strategy was sound, is irresponsible and fruitless. As Towsend Hoopes wrote:

> Until the Viet Cong infrastructure was rooted out of the countryside and the population persuaded to acknowledge and support, if not quite to love, the government in Saigon, large-scale victories over NVN forces would be inherently inconclusive. Moreover, large-scale victories involved artillery and air strikes which killed civilians and thus inhibited political persuasion.[10]

Regarding the immensity of the military factors in that area of the world, Army Chief of Staff General George H. Decker said:

> We cannot win a conventional war in Southeast Asia. If we go in, we should go in to win, and that means bombing Hanoi, China, and maybe even using nuclear weapons.[11]

Lyndon Johnson and Robert McNamara did want to go in to win—but they never could and never did define winning. They never totally understood that military victory could not be achieved without political stability in South Vietnam. The only way to win was to protect the people of South Vietnam. This was clearly beyond our capability.

Had President Kennedy lived, maybe he would not have followed the strictly traditional, full-blown military strategy approved by President Johnson and Secretary McNamara. It was massive in scope but could never be decisive enough to be effective because the all-important ground operations focused on fire power instead of people. It is interesting that Robert S. McNamara, who prided himself so much on the logic of efficiency, ended up approving such an inefficient and illogical strategy. McNamara was the expert who never made a small mistake on his way to the grand fallacy. Chester L. Cooper summarized Secretary McNamara's dedication to false principles:

> In 1962 McNamara was at the American Pacific Headquarters in Honolulu, and after a briefing by General Harkins he said, "Now General, show me a graph that will tell me whether we are losing or winning in Vietnam." By 1967 the numbers may have been accurate, relevant, and correctly interpreted, but few really believed them.[12]

There were many different strategies that we could have selected in Vietnam.

• We could have declared war on North Vietnam and then invaded and tried to occupy that country. If achievable, on the plus side this would have been the most effective and efficient way to stop the North from invading the South. The negative side was the distinct possibility of starting a war with China or the Soviet Union or maybe both. To complicate matters, we sent the North Vietnamese the critically devastating message that we would not invade their country. As General Palmer wrote:

> President Johnson, beginning in 1965, let it be known to North Vietnamese leaders that the United States did not intend to invade North Vietnam or otherwise try to bring down the Hanoi government. Thereafter, U. S. actions without exception reaffirmed that impression of U. S. intent. This practically sealed South Vietnam's doom, for it allowed Hanoi complete freedom to employ all its forces in the South.[13]

• We could have tried to defend only the key areas of South Vietnam. This was the enclave concept outlined by General James M. Gavin in the February 1966 issue of *Harper's* magazine. The positive side is that this strategy was designed to protect the populated areas of South Vietnam. In addition, it might have given the South Vietnamese the time needed to achieve a popular government. The negative is that our involvement could have been indefinite. Tristram Coffin wrote:

> General Gavin's solution was quite simple. Hang on to what we had, including the big urban complexes, to show the enemy we could not be driven out. Lay off the extravagant bombings. Avoid escalation. Seek a political settlement.[14]

• We could have kept our involvement at the adviser level and let the South Vietnamese fight or not fight for their country. The plus here is that we would have kept our involvement limited. The negative is the South Vietnamese probably could not have been successful on their own because their government lacked popular backing.

• We could have tried to use our military forces efficiently by limiting their use exclusively to prevent the North Vietnamese from infiltrating into South Vietnam directly from North Vietnam and from Laos and Cambodia. The big plus here is that we would not have been fighting a war of attrition and we would not have taken over the war from the South Vietnamese. The negative side is that our troops might not have been able to stop infiltration from the North. With this strategy we also could not have prevented Viet Cong recruitment in South Vietnam. In addition, politically and militarily, South Vietnam might just not have been able to make it as a country.

As Douglas Kinnard wrote:

> Even in 1967 it was not too late to change the basic strategy, i.e. employ most United States forces in the north (including Laos) to insulate South Vietnam from the North. At the same time put a massive effort into upgrading the South Vietnamese forces for their task of wearing down the VC—who would no longer be constantly reinforced, reindoctrinated, retrained, and resupplied from the North.[15]

• The strategy we picked not only kept North Vietnam safe from invasion but also enabled them to use the Ho Chi Minh Trail to infiltrate from North Vietnam, Laos, and Cambodia. To compensate for our inability to invade North Vietnam, our military strategy included heavy bombing of a backward agricultural country. Finally, to fight a guerrilla-type land war in Asia, the army selected a strategy of attrition. As we painfully found out, there were no positives to this strategy. It left all the advantages to the enemy, a fact that should have been a sign to our civilian leaders that something was fundamentally wrong. Andrew F. Krepinevich, Jr., wrote:

> Simply stated, having failed over the past decade to produce forces and doctrine capable of executing a counterinsurgency strategy, the army was trying to fit a strategy to its force structure and doctrine.[16]

It was a mess that started from the McNamara concept of "gradual response," the idea of applying military power in small increments first and then adding more and more force until success would be achieved. The JCS never believed in gradual response, but they were never asked. Had the president controlled the situation, he would have sat down with the JCS—all of them—noted service objections and avoided the fatal trap.

As unbelievable as it may sound, we initially followed this strategy of gradual response with the bombing of North Vietnam, which enabled the enemy to build anti-aircraft batteries while we held back. Eventually, as described by Admiral Moorer, Air Force Chief of Staff John P. McConnell, and Admiral Sharp, commander-in-chief in the Pacific, we paid with the needless loss of American lives when the order came to knock out the anti-aircraft batteries so massive bombing could continue.

Robert Donovan summarized the negatives of gradual response:

> Unfortunately, Vietnam, with its difficult terrain, civil war passions, and logistical assistance to the enemy from the Chinese and the Soviets, was the worst place imaginable for testing the concept of gradual response.[17]

Regarding our decision to fight a war of attrition (search and destroy), General Bruce Palmer wrote:

> Hanoi's available resources were clearly adequate to sustain the war indefinitely.[18]

The psychological dimension—paralyzing a nation's confidence and will to fight—is important in any war. Our only hope in Vietnam, considering the limitations we were under, would have been to hit the enemy with everything we had as quickly as we could. Unfortunately, the strategy of "gradual response" selected by our civilian leaders was the opposite. Caspar Weinberger said:

> In those cases where our national interests require us to commit combat forces, we must never let there be doubt of our resolution. When it is necessary for our troops to be committed to combat, we *must* commit them in sufficient numbers, and we *must* support them as effectively and resolutely as our strength permits. When we commit our troops to combat we must do so with the sole object of winning.[19]

• We could have chosen not to get involved because it was, in the end, a political civil war beyond our ability even to understand. If none of our European allies were willing to get involved, then maybe it was hopeless. As we were to learn the hard way, the United States cannot afford to involve its military without congressional involvement and with a political strategy designed to win—no matter what. At an August 31, 1963, meeting, Paul Kattenburg, director of the Interdepartmental Vietnam Task Force, was:

> . . . dismayed by the administration's ignorance of Vietnam, its recent history, and the personalities and forces in contention there. . . . Believing that Kennedy's advisers (McNamara and Taylor) "were leading themselves down a garden path to tragedy," Kattenburg then blurted out the unthinkable: "At this juncture, it would be better for us to make the decision to get out honorably."[20]

The military, I believe, also sensed that unless we were determined to win, it would be best not to go in at all. Outlining the basic views of Army Chief of Staff Harold Johnson, General Palmer stated:

> As the Vietnam crisis deepened, the JCS and the services debated and discussed at great length the question of the

U. S. commitment. General Johnson, perhaps the most knowledgeable and understanding of any American leader on Vietnam, often remarked that if the United States was not willing to "go all the way," that is, to include direct confrontation with the Soviet Union and China, who supplied Hanoi with the means to attack the South, then we had best not go in at all. But the problem was to delineate just where our interests lay in Southeast Asia and to define U. S. objectives—specifically, what we were trying to do in South Vietnam.[21]

Out of all of this, President Johnson and the army ended up trying to fight World War II initially against the Viet Cong and then against a highly mobile North Vietnamese Army. He should have reread the words of President Kennedy:

> This is another type of war, new in its intensity, ancient in its origin—war by guerrillas, subversives, insurgents, combat by infiltration, instead of aggression, seeking victory by eroding and exhausting the enemy instead of engaging him. . . . It requires a whole new kind of strategy, a whole different kind of military training.[22]

The absolute worst thing we could have done in Vietnam was to fight a war of attrition. Our civilian leaders never should have allowed it to happen. Politically, it could not be sustained in the United States, and on the battlefield, it gave the enemy the advantage of fighting *his* war. It would have been like Robert E. Lee trying to fight a war of attrition against General Grant. Douglas Kinnard summarized the facts:

> But one thing should be made absolutely clear: attrition is not a strategy. It is irrefutable proof of the absence of any strategy. A commander who resorts to attrition admits his failure to conceive of an alternative. He turns from warfare as an art and accepts it on the most nonprofessional terms imaginable. He uses blood in lieu of brains. Saying that political considerations forced the

employment of attrition warfare does not alter the hard truth that the United States was strategically bankrupt in Vietnam.[23]

President Kennedy understood the military reality of Vietnam, the fact that it was initially a guerrilla as well as a political type of war we were involved in, not one that could be won by using large numbers of combat troops in the inefficient way we did. He stressed many times to people like General Maxwell Taylor that he would not use American combat troops in Vietnam. He always kept in mind the critical distinction between advisers and combat troops. He understood that it was ultimately the South Vietnamese who had to fight for their country. It was that simple. Speaking to Walter Cronkite, Kennedy said:

> We are prepared to continue to assist them, but I don't think that the war can be won unless the people support the effort and, in my opinion, in the last two months, the government has gotten out of touch with the people.
>
> In the final analysis, it's their war. They're the ones who have to win it or lose it. We can help them, give them equipment, we can send our men out there as advisers, but they have to win it, the people of Vietnam, against the Communists.[24]

Unfortunately, the crucial distinction between advisers and combat troops got lost when President Kennedy died. When we moved from advisers to combat troops, we never understood what the consequences would be, both in South Vietnam and at home, by our taking over the war. We did not project ourselves into the future to ask:

- What would be the consequences of our taking over the military part of the war from the South Vietnamese?
- Did the strategy we selected enable us to protect the people of South Vietnam?
- What was the long-term meaning of South Vietnam not having a government that represented the people?

• Did it make sense to go in without a single major ally?

• In other words, did we expect to win? Were we going to kill every single North Vietnamese who came into South Vietnam, first, as the Viet Cong and, later, as organized combat units?

• How did we expect South Vietnam to finally govern itself—or were we going to eventually take on this task also?

What seems clear is that we had the objective of preventing North Vietnam from taking over South Vietnam but no political or military strategy for doing it. We just assumed we could win because we were the powerful United States. We thought the issue always was what should we do instead of should we do anything. We never defined what winning was nor did we ever consider losing. Maxwell Taylor said:

> As we became more deeply involved there was little thought given to the additional cost we would have to pay if, after trying, we then failed. This cost of failure increased as time went on.[25]

Civilian leaders like Lyndon Johnson, Robert McNamara, McGeorge Bundy, and Walter Rostow made the mistake of defining Vietnam as critical to the United States and, therefore, under any conditions, worth fighting for regardless of what the American people believed. As Robert McNamara said on January 27, 1964:

> The survival of an independent government in South Vietnam is so important to the security of Southeast Asia and to the free world that I can conceive of no alternative than to take all necessary measures within our capability to prevent a Communist victory.[26]

Robert McNamara was right; he could conceive of "no alternatives." His was a personality that considered the alternatives of others a threat when, in fact, he should have looked to many sources to get alternatives that made sense. To find the best answers to any problem, you need a process based on creating and evaluating alternatives. Admiral Moorer said:

> It is important, in my view, that the president of the United States receive not just a single recommendation but rather options as to what would be the best course of action from which we would choose.[27]

This is precisely why the Goldwater-Nichols Act, which focuses so much on the JCS chairman, will prove to be so wrong. Let's hope the mistake, when it comes, will not be as colossal as Vietnam.

The facts are, out of all our key civilian leaders, only President Kennedy initially understood the limits of our military capability considering the army's inability to effectively fight a low-intensity conflict. As William Rust has written:

> Throughout the Kennedy and Johnson administrations, the Joint Chiefs of Staff faced the problem of policymakers' objectives and rhetoric exceeding the military means they were willing to employ.[28]

Our political leaders were unclear on what they were doing, and they closed off alternatives by making statements with no strategy to back them. Eventually, the American people ended up confused and without reason to support our war effort. But I do believe the American people were smart enough to sense the illogic of our taking over the war. Colonel Harry G. Summers, Jr., wrote:

> Our inability to explain in clear and understandable language what we were about in Vietnam undercut American support for the war.[29]

So what we should never have let happen is our taking over the war from the South Vietnamese. If they did not want to fight because they could not identify with their own government, then nothing could be done. Our political leaders should have understood the dominant political dimension of the situation in Vietnam. Towsend Hoopes wrote:

> Sooner or later, and probably sooner, the American people would reawaken to the fact that they were still committed to the endless support of a group of men in Saigon who represented nobody but themselves, preferred war to the risks of a political settlement, and could not remain in power for more than a few months without our large-scale presence.[30]

As we had defined it, this political war was not militarily winnable by us alone. If we wanted to make it a purely military matter, then we had to invade North Vietnam. This would have been the surest way to achieve the strategic offensive. By limiting our ground troop involvement to South Vietnam, we were always on the strategic defensive militarily while achieving nothing of political value to the South Vietnamese. To do this the army would have had to defend the people by fighting a counterinsurgency war in the South. Andrew F. Krepinevich, Jr., wrote:

> Thus, in Vietnam the army ended up trying to fight the kind of conventional war that it was trained, organized, and preferred (and that it wanted) to fight instead of the counterinsurgency war it was sent to fight.[31]

We could not win the war in Vietnam without a declaration of war by Congress and a total mobilization of the country. I don't believe the American people would have supported this kind of total commitment. James Clay Thompson wrote:

> American policies failed in Vietnam because the most striking characteristic of these policies after the buildup of American forces was the imbalance between policy goals and the means available to reach those ends. . . . First, domestic political opposition ruled out a general mobilization of the American population and economy. Second, fear of escalation into a vastly larger war with the People's Republic of China or a nuclear confrontation

> with the Soviet Union limited the kind of force that could be brought to bear in Indochina. American policies failed, then, because of a basic contradiction between ends and means and an inability to abandon unattainable goals.[32]

While researching our Vietnamese involvement, I was surprised to find out that, as I said earlier, President Kennedy made such a sharp and wise distinction between advisers and combat troops as President Eisenhower had done before him. He said in 1962 that before sending in combat troops he would go to Congress.

Here is what Chester Cooper wrote:

> On the same day the president took pains to point out that although there were "a good many Americans" in Vietnam, they were no "combat troops." If American troops were to go into combat, Kennedy said, "I, of course, would go to Congress."[33]

President Johnson was not willing to go to Congress for a declaration of war, which I don't believe would have helped unless we were willing to risk invading North Vietnam. The fact that the administration was unwilling to come to Congress for a declaration of war, along with the noninvolvement of any of our European allies, should have prompted Congress, at this point, to get involved. It was their responsibility to alert the American people to what was happening. The American people should have been asked for their approval before we proceeded.

Caspar Weinberger has cautioned:

> When we ask our military forces to risk their very lives—a note of caution is not only prudent, it is morally required.[34]

Instead, President Johnson was able to use the Tonkin Gulf Resolution of August 7, 1964, as a substitute for a declaration of war. Congress should not have let him get away with this dangerous distortion of the Constitution. Because Congress has the right to declare war, it must be involved whenever American troops are committed. Hence, Congress must consider legislation that would prevent the possibility of something like the Gulf of Tonkin Resolution from ever happening again. Remember, on August 4, 1964, Commodore Herrick, Maddox/Turner Joy Task group commander, said this about the supposed attack:

> Review of action makes many recorded contacts and torpedoes fired appear doubtful. Freak weather effects and overeager sonarmen may have accounted for many reports. No actual visual sightings by Maddox. Suggest complete evaluation before any further action.[35]

Admiral Jim Stockdale, who was flying over the Tonkin Gulf on August 4, said quite emphatically in his book, *In Love and War,* that absolutely nothing happened. Yet not knowing the truth, Congress overwhelmingly passed the Tonkin Gulf Resolution.

Surely the War Powers Act is no answer because it gives the president the right to use the military, initially, without *any* congressional involvement whatsoever. Any sensible person must recognize the possible dangerous consequences of the War Powers Act, particularly when considering a powerful chairman who can manipulate a president. Here the force of the Goldwater-Nichols Act, coupled with the War Powers Act, will institutionalize the Gulf of Tonkin Resolution. Nothing could be more unconstitutional or more dangerous.

In Vietnam we ended up with the political and military initiative belonging to the enemy. There were reasons for this, reasons that our civilian leaders should have understood, anticipated, and been guided by. Said simply, the North Vietnamese were not a bunch of nice guys, but they were fighting a "revolutionary" war designed to unite their country and to keep colonial powers like France and the United States out. The war in Vietnam was not a simple matter of the North invading the South. The elements of a civil war were clearly evident. I am not saying that we should not have tried to help the South Vietnamese. Strategically, I believe it would have been right—but not by our taking over the war. Caspar Weinberger said:

> Recent history has proven that we cannot assume unilaterally the role of the world's defender. We have learned that there are limits to how much of our spirit and blood and treasure we can afford to forfeit in meeting our responsibility to keep peace and freedom. So while we may and should offer substantial amounts of economic and military assistance to our allies in their time of need, and help them maintain forces to deter attacks against them—usually we cannot substitute our troops or our will for theirs.[36]

The population of both North and South Vietnam feared *any* outside colonial power and, surely, the people of South Vietnam could not distinguish between the United States and the French, who had been in Indochina for so long. There was just no understandable way for the people of Vietnam to see the United States as the good guys, separated from the long involvement of the French in Indochina.

Directly or indirectly, the people of Vietnam knew the United States had financed the French involvement in Vietnam in the 1950s. For example, from 1950 to 1954 the United States paid 80 percent of the cost for the French military in Vietnam. Chester Cooper wrote:

> Altogether, between early 1950 and the end of the war in the spring of 1954, the United States supplied the French with $2.6 billion of military material—about 80 percent of the cost of the French military effort.[37]

President Roosevelt was right when he made it quite clear at the Allied conference held during World War II that he didn't want the French or any other major power returning to Indochina after the war. He knew colonialism would not work any longer in Indochina because it opposed the momentum of history. A new way had to be found. He believed the key would be the United Nations. Tristram Coffin wrote:

Roosevelt strongly opposed a French return to its holdings, and wanted Indochina set-up under a United Nations trusteeship, and free of big power control.[38]

How shocked President Roosevelt would have been to know that it was the French who tried to return, and that when the French failed, it was the United States of America who replaced the French—without United Nations backing and without the support of a single major ally.

The political reality we were faced with was a united North Vietnam fighting a war of revolution under Ho Chi Minh, and South Vietnam being a government that was, at best, incompetent and, at worst, corrupt. The United States tried to use a massive army restricted to the South to solve this dangerously complicated political situation.

General Dave Richard Palmer put it perfectly by saying:

> It was the awareness, at long last, that purely military solutions could never defeat the insurgency. Diem and his advisers came to realize that they were fighting a political war as well as a military one. Saigon finally saw that the populace had to be separated from the insurgents and that real social reform was necessary to counter the enemy's appeal.[39]

For the United States to misunderstand initially the true nature of the war was an error that must be shared by the executive branch, the military, and Congress. We must find ways for making sure serious mistakes, like misunderstanding the political dimension of the situation in Vietnam, can never happen again. The Goldwater-Nichols Act does nothing to help this issue. What we need is a reevaluation of how the executive branch and Congress work together to define our foreign policy objectives. The current system, whereby the executive branch makes decisions and the Congress just waits for mistakes to happen before it acts, is no good. Congress must be made a more active, positive player in foreign policy decision making.

Yes, North Vietnam ended up being quite irrational and, by

any standard, brutal and imperialistic. It was not then and is not now the kind of nation to bring stability and freedom to the region, particularly considering the invasion of Cambodia. Soviet control of the port of Cam Ranh Bay is a real strategic loss to the United States in the Pacific. However, the question should never have been whether or not the North Vietnamese were good guys or not. The issue should have been whether or not we at least understood what they were doing and why; to ask ourselves from a strategic viewpoint what precisely could have been achieved. Could we fight a limited war while the North Vietnamese were willing to pay any price to achieve "unconditional surrender"? Robert Donovan:

> While the president was fighting a limited war more than nine thousand miles away, the North Vietnamese were waging total war on their own soil with tactics suited to their jungles and mountains and perfected over centuries of fighting foreign domination.[40]

In reality the United States went to war to defend an illusion. South Vietnam was not a country. This crucial fact should have been clear to our civilian leaders. In order to fight communism, we simply could not demand that South Vietnam be what we wanted to imagine. South Vietnam was a place with people trying to decide what they wanted to be with no government they could commit themselves to. The one similarity with our revolutionary war was that our allies could and did help but, ultimately, we had to be responsible for fighting the war ourselves. We were able to unite because we believed in our government and in ourselves. The power of revolution was with the American people. This was not so in Vietnam. Robert J. Donovan:

> The United States went to the defense of a nation that was not really a nation in the sense understood by Americans.[41]

What our civilian leaders should have been asking themselves is What do we want to accomplish and can it be done? In

1954 and again in 1956, President Eisenhower decided not to go into Vietnam because we could not win and because none of our allies were willing to fight. As Eisenhower decided, based on the well-thought-out advice of Army Chief of Staff General Matthew B. Ridgway, for the United States to go in alone was irresponsible madness. Even if we had won militarily, the political structure needed to make South Vietnam a country was not there. CIA director Vice Admiral William Raborn said:

> There is little point in spending U. S. lives and treasure to obtain a conference or a settlement which, in the absence of a viable non-Communist state, must lead either to U. S. reintervention or a subsequent Communist takeover.[42]

It should serve as a warning, regarding what can happen even under the old law, that General Ridgway had trouble getting to President Eisenhower because Chairman of the Joint Chiefs Arthur W. Radford was in favor of our getting involved in Vietnam.

At the time of the French fall at Dienbienphu in 1954, President Eisenhower made it quite clear that without allies we would not consider going in. Chester Cooper wrote:

> Eisenhower recounts that he immediately telephoned Bedell Smith [then undersecretary of state] about the French request for direct intervention and "agreed that Foster's [Dulles] position should stand unchanged. There would be no intervention without allies."[43]

Nobody wanted to prevent the Communists from taking over all of Indochina more than John Foster Dulles. But the limits of what could be accomplished were clear. On May 25, 1954, Secretary Dulles said:

> We are not prepared to go in for a defense of colonialism. We are only going to go in for a defense of liberty. . . . We don't go in alone; we go in where the other nations which

> have an important stake in the area recognize the peril as we do. We go in where the United Nations gives moral sanctions to our actions.[44]

In 1954 Senator Kennedy paralleled what Secretary Dulles was saying.

> The hard truth of the matter is . . . that without the whole-hearted support of the peoples of the associated states, without a reliable and crusading native army with a dependable officer corps, a military victory, even with American support, in that area is difficult if not impossible [to achieve].[45]

At no time from the end of World War II on did we ever understand what was going on in Indochina and, therefore, what kind of commitment it would take to achieve the result we wanted. We never understood precisely what was in our long-term interest—and, most important, what was achievable. We reacted and we reacted with increasingly less perspective.

Even President Truman's initial decision to get us involved with the French was made with limited understanding. He just wanted to stop communism—and, as we were to find out, you can't run foreign policy without seeing clearly the limits of your capability. General Bruce Palmer said:

> In retrospect it seems clear that the Truman administration's decision to begin military aid for Indochina was taken in more or less instinctive support of the U. S. umbrella policy of containment everywhere in the world without much regard for the merits of each case and, in this instance, with little knowledge of the Indochina situation.[46]

Our military was rigid in its thinking and unable to understand the real situation that would be faced in the field. We kept thinking in terms of our World War II and Korea experiences where large armies fought each other head on. This experience had no relevance to Vietnam, and we never understood the critical importance of Laos and Cambodia in the total picture. If we could not stop North Vietnamese infiltration through these countries, then our military strategy was indeed flawed. Douglas Kinnard summarized the infiltration problem:

> A second area of constraints covered cross-border operations into North Vietnam, Laos, and Cambodia. It was well known that the North Vietnamese line of communications went through neighboring countries and that Hanoi had established base areas contiguous to the South Vietnamese border. Nevertheless, for much of the war the United States did not operate with its ground troops in those areas—in effect, giving the enemy sanctuaries in which he could operate. As a result, in the period of 1965 to May 1970 the enemy had the great advantage of being able to fight the war his way. The reasons for this restraint have to do with attempts to avoid a bigger war and to accommodate public opinion at home and abroad.[47]

Our incorrect tactical thinking had a great influence on the South Vietnamese military, especially because we controlled the supplies and were supposed to be experts at fighting wars. Instead of building a counterinsurgence mobile capability, they were forced to build a World War II-type army. This was to have tragic results both militarily and politically because the people saw that the South Vietnamese military could not protect them. Again, General Palmer:

> Failing to grasp the nature of the total threat, U.S. leaders initially perceived the major threat to be an overt, across-the-border invasion by North Vietnamese or Chinese forces, and were slow in recognizing the serious threat posed by subversion, infiltration, and guerrilla warfare.[48]

The facts are the American army had no idea whatsoever about how to effectively fight a guerrilla war. Somehow they wanted to believe that if war came, we could deal with it as we always did. This kind of 1940s thinking was dangerous indeed. In addition, our incorrect strategic thinking assumed that if things got real tough, we could somehow rely on the atomic bomb. This simplistic thinking was to cost us dearly in Vietnam. Dave Richard Palmer:

> Though it may seem utterly unbelievable, it is nonetheless true that the Pentagon had to order a crash, army-wide campaign to reeducate its officers. Steeped in conventional theory and oriented towards an atomic war in Europe, many professional officers did not even recognize the term "counterinsurgency," much less were they prepared to practice it.[49]

To our nonexistent political strategy for victory we added the wrong military strategy. Therefore, the United States had no chance to achieve its goal in Vietnam because the plan to win was not applicable to the problem. Many years too late and with the advantage of hindsight, Senator J. William Fulbright summarized the situation:

> What I do question is the ability of the United States, or France or any other Western nation, to go into a small, alien, undeveloped Asian nation and create stability where there is chaos, the will to fight where there is defeatism, democracy where there is no tradition of it and honest government where corruption is almost a way of life.[50]

When President-elect John F. Kennedy met with President Eisenhower to discuss Indochina in late 1960, only Laos was mentioned. This is where President Eisenhower expected that we would have to make our stand—not Vietnam. Understandably, because much of the new president's time was spent on areas such as Cuba and Berlin, he was late in putting significant attention on Vietnam.

I am firmly convinced that it would not have been possible for his advisers to convince President Kennedy to approve getting us involved in a full-fledged war in Vietnam, involving masses of combat troops so inefficiently and ineffectively. Robert J. Donovan:

> While broadening American commitment with money, equipment, military advisers, and pilots, Kennedy did not accept the proposal from his own advisers for deployment of combat forces.[51]

President Kennedy was desperately trying to find a way to prevent South Vietnam from falling to the Communists—there is no question about this. But he did believe the South Vietnamese had to win the war themselves—he was not going to give them any blank checks.

From 1961 to November 1963 there were people in the administration, like Secretary of Defense Robert S. McNamara and Chairman of the Joint Chiefs of Staff General Maxwell D. Taylor, who kept recommending to the president that we get involved with combat troops. But on each occasion President Kennedy made it clear that he would not. In fact, he always preserved the option of getting out.

Just before his death Kennedy said to White House aide Michael Forrestal, who was leaving on a trip to Cambodia:

> When you come back, I want you to organize an in-depth study of every possible option we've got in Vietnam, including how to get out of there. We have to review this whole thing from the bottom to the top.[52]

Just before he left for Texas, President Kennedy called Senator Wayne Morse, who was strongly against the war. He informed the senator about his decision to have a full review of our policy in Vietnam.

The irony of the situation is that President Diem did not want American combat troops. He wanted our help but he was smart enough to know that once we took over the war, all would be lost. William Rust:

> Although Diem welcomed additional military advisers and equipment, he did not want U.S. combat troops.[53]

President Diem knew that the key to winning was having a strong South Vietnam, first politically and then militarily. He knew that once the U.S. took over, his country would indeed be helpless. This is exactly what happened. I don't believe President Johnson or any of his other civilian advisers ever understood the true significance of our taking over the war. It is interesting that General Taylor, who had recommended the use of American combat troops, had obviously changed his mind. Robert J. Donovan:

> Taylor had warned Johnson against such a deployment. Once the policy against committing ground forces had been breached, the ambassador cabled, it would be "very difficult to hold the line on future deployments. . . . Intervention with ground forces would at best buy time and would lead to ever-increasing commitments until, like the French, we would be occupying an essentially hostile foreign country."[54]

What Lyndon Johnson tried to do by putting over 500,000 troops into Vietnam was substitute American lives for his lack of a strategy. To then use these troops in a war of attrition in Asia, of all places, defies all logic. Even today Vietnam has a very large army, among the top five in the world. We had it backwards: manpower was not North Vietnam's problem—it was our problem. The decision to send 500,000 troops was not based on anything military. It was simply the figure General Westmoreland estimated we could get away with without having to resort to total mobilization. Douglas Kinnard wrote:

> Westmoreland at one point had his staff in Saigon make their own estimate of the highest troop strength the United States could support in Vietnam without a mobilization. Their answer was a half-million men. This, rather than any specific strategic or tactical plan, was the

> basis of the manpower goal which the Military Assistance Command sought. . . . If the foregoing seems to indicate more preoccupation in Washington with how many troops were needed and the amount that could be provided rather than why they were needed, this is what the record shows.[55]

The question then is How can we prevent something like this from ever happening again? President Johnson was essentially out of control with his primary focus being on military detail instead of the more important issue of political grand strategy and oversight. He and Secretary McNamara confused their ultimate responsibility for our military direction with who should be doing it. Civilians in our form of government are responsible for both policy formation and military execution. However, it is the military who must actually recommend and then be responsible for how we fight. Civilians then judge the result and make changes if necessary. President Johnson became his own military czar and with no declaration of war by the Congress. He worked with a very narrow group, including Secretary McNamara and Chairman of the Joint Chiefs Earle Wheeler. Vietnam is a clear example of what happens when a president deals only with the JCS chairman.

No American president must ever be allowed to do something like this again. The Goldwater-Nichols Act is silent on the critical issue involving the need for direct congressional involvement, particularly at the beginning of the process. President Johnson hoped, somehow, that if we did more of the same, then at some point it had to work. As a *Saturday Evening Post* editorial said:

> The war in Vietnam is Johnson's mistake and, through the power of his office, he has made it a national mistake.[56]

Based on what happened I believe it would have been essential for President Johnson to be seeing *all* the chiefs, not just

McNamara and General Wheeler. Under the Goldwater-Nichols Act we are making this mistake the law of the land.

According to presidential military aide General Chester V. Clifton, President Johnson thought it was McNamara's job to deal with the Joint Chiefs of Staff as a body, unlike President Kennedy, who made it policy to meet with *all* the chiefs once a month. This may very well have been the biggest mistake of the war. Admiral Moorer:

> In my opinion, none of the last several presidents met with the Joint Chiefs on an eye-to-eye basis as often as necessary.[57]

What the Goldwater-Nichols Act does is institutionalize this serious mistake. From now on, as the JCS chairman grows in power, it will be easier and easier for a president and a chairman of the Joint Chiefs to run any American war. In time, of course, we risk a situation where the chairman alone can first run a war and then, as drastic as it sounds now, the whole country.

Let's now consider the role of the Joint Chiefs in the Vietnam tragedy. The complete details are hard to pinpoint, but we do know:

• McNamara had a destructive, adversarial relationship with the chiefs. He kept trying to do their job. He never understood his crucial role as a political leader.

• Many people disagreed with General Westmoreland's search and destroy tactic of attrition, yet neither Johnson, McNamara, nor the chiefs did anything to either change the strategy or to have Westmoreland replaced. General Palmer wrote:

> In short, there seems to have been insufficient timely discussion in Washington as to how and for what purpose U.S. forces were to be employed in South Vietnam, that is, the U.S. strategy to be pursued in conducting the crucial ground war in a decisive way.[58]

Towsend Hoopes:

> Yet the president never insisted on a comparable overview of Westmoreland's operations, nor did McNamara.[59]

This is a devastating condemnation of Johnson and McNamara as political leaders. They started a momentum without understanding the true implications of what they had done. They should have been working closely with all the chiefs and with key members of Congress to develop alternate, achievable objectives—including the possibility of not going in with combat troops. For Lyndon Johnson to use the Tonkin Gulf Resolution as a congressional declaration of war was one of the true low points in American history. It was a clear distortion of the Constitution with devastating consequences. Harry G. Summers, Jr., wrote:

> The requirements for a declaration of war were rooted in the principle of civilian control of the military, and the failure to declare war in Vietnam drove a wedge between the army and large segments of the American public.[60]

I believe the fact that President Johnson did not work regularly with all the chiefs at least in part explains why the advice he received from the chiefs was not the best. The Goldwater-Nichols Act tries to fix this situation by further limiting the advice and alternatives given to the president. I believe it would be better to do the opposite and make it *mandatory* for the president to meet regularly with all the chiefs and with congressional leaders. General Palmer:

> Finally, there was one glaring omission in the advice the JCS provided the president and the secretary of defense. It is an obvious omission, but more important, a profoundly significant one. Not once during the war did the JCS advise the commander-in-chief or the secretary of defense that the strategy being pursued most probably would fail and that the United States would be unable to

> achieve its objectives. The only explanation of this failure is that the chiefs were involved with the "can do" spirit and could not bring themselves to make such a negative statement or to appear to be disloyal.[61]

The other part of the problem had to do with the defects in Lyndon Johnson's personality. Johnson was a man who clearly never should have been president or, more pertinently, commander-in-chief. Robert Donovan describes it this way:

> Johnson was a tragic political genius of bottomless pettiness, volcanic energy, brilliant intellect, disgusting manners, wild emotions, voracious appetites, habitual mendacity, restless cunning, nagging insecurity, great achievements, and sometimes near lunacy.[62]

All the more reason why we must make sure we have the checks and balances needed to prevent a president like Johnson from getting totally out of control. The best way is to have effective congressional involvement, not to increase the power of the chairman of the Joint Chiefs of Staff.

President Roosevelt would not have gotten involved in military meddling. He would have instead fired McNamara and probably Westmoreland as he did Admiral Kimmel and General Short after Pearl Harbor. Why? Because in war, there are mistakes which cannot be accepted. A president can take no chances with the lives of brave Americans for whom he is ultimately responsible. As secretary of defense Caspar W. Weinberger said in a Veterans Day ceremony speech on November 11, 1986, at Arlington Cemetery:

> We must insure that no American views war casually nor talks cavalierly about the commitment of U.S. forces abroad.

In the final analysis the American people could not forgive Johnson's incompetence and irresponsible behavior.

Towsend Hoopes wrote:

> What seemed in retrospect to have made large-scale military intervention all but inevitable in 1965 was a fateful combination of the president's uncertainty and sense of insecurity in handling foreign policy, and a prevailing set of assumptions among his close advisers that reinforced his own tendency to think about the external world in the simplistic terms of appeasement versus military resolve. . . . For reasons which seemed to have their roots deep in his personal history, he lacked the kind of confidence in his own judgment that permitted Truman, Eisenhower, and Kennedy to overrule their principal foreign policy and military advisers on major issues. In matters of war and peace he seemed too much the sentimental patriot, lacking Truman's practical horse sense, Eisenhower's experienced caution, Kennedy's cool grasp of reality.[63]

I am sure John F. Kennedy would have given more thought to who his vice president should have been if he had known what was going to happen. I hope all future presidential nominees make sure the person they select to run with them will be, above all else, a political leader with the talent and, most important, the character to be president.

General Palmer gave a clear insight of Lyndon Johnson as a leader:

> The first meeting was especially disconcerting for two reasons. First, the presidential photographer was present the entire time, taking an unending series of snapshots of the president from every conceivable angle. It was impossible to ignore the photographer's presence. Second, the president was in constant motion, receiving or making telephone calls, pressing the buzzer under the top of the desk to give orders for all kinds of tasks, and frequently interrupting anyone trying to articulate his views. The atmosphere was hardly conducive to a meaningful discussion.[64]

From an overall political viewpoint, the big mistakes of the war were never asking ourselves whether or not we should be involved and why; looking for alternative ways of helping South Vietnam that would not have resulted in our taking over the war; and not understanding clearly what it meant to fight a low-intensity, counterinsurgency war. If we had decided not to fight a counterinsurgency war, then we had to declare war and get ready to invade North Vietnam.

By having neither a political strategy nor a ground strategy and by not declaring war, the military was in a no-win position in Vietnam. Surely the army did not help by trying to win the war with search and destroy ground operations, nor did it make sense for us to resort to massive bombing of the North with the expectations we had. James Clay Thompson wrote:

> In retrospect, the failure of senior American decision makers in the spring of 1965 to appreciate the weakness of strategic air power as a weapon must be judged as a colossal mistake in political-military judgment.[65]

The existence of the atomic bomb had a significant effect on our Vietnam strategy. It resulted in our not considering an invasion of North Vietnam because we feared a conventional war with China or the Soviet Union or possibly a nuclear war with the Soviet Union. We learned from the Korean War the risk in going near the Chinese or Soviet borders. However, our civilian leaders never learned what it meant to fight a guerrilla-type war in Vietnam.

Regarding the Joint Chiefs of Staff, the major player in the war was Chairman of the Joint Chiefs of Staff General Earle D. Wheeler. I would describe General Wheeler as a weak chairman which, considering their personalities, would be exactly what President Johnson and Secretary McNamara would have wanted. A strong chairman might have helped but would not have been the answer.

The answer would have been for *all* the chiefs to be intimately involved with all that went on; to be running their services as leaders in the chain of command, not as advisers. Then, as a logical extension of this authority, the chiefs must also be responsible for what happens in the field. It is at this point that our military effectiveness has been breaking down time and again since World War II. This command involvement from Washington will not hurt the unified and specified commanders, it will help. Said simply, the chiefs must be responsible for determining worldwide military strategy and for making sure it is effectively carried out. Admiral Moorer:

> Those who make the plans have got to be responsible for the execution.[66]

Total political and military unity of command must be at the presidential level—not at the level of the secretary of defense or, surely, not at the JCS chairman's level.

The president and the country would have benefited by having the secretary of defense and all the chiefs working closely together to present the pros and cons of alternate recommendations. We should have gotten away from the outdated tradition that the man in the field should have the final say in what gets done. Tactically, this logic does apply but not under all conditions; strategically, it surely does not.

For example, the chiefs and the secretary of defense should have evaluated Westmoreland's search and destroy strategy of attrition and made recommendations of alternative strategies to the president. Leaving strategy to the field commander was wrong, and it will always be wrong. That is why we must be very careful about making the unified and specified commanders islands unto themselves, which is what the Goldwater-Nichols Act does.

I could not disagree more strongly with what President Truman said about our decision to go beyond the 38th Parallel in Korea:

> What we should have done is stop at the neck of Korea right here (pointing to a globe). . . . That's what the British wanted. . . . We knew the Chinese had close to a million men on the border and all that. . . . But (MacArthur) was commander in the field. You pick your man, you've got to back him up. That's the only way a military

> organization can work. I got the best advice I could and the man on the spot said this was the thing to do . . . so I agreed. That was my decision—no matter what hindsight shows.[67]

President Truman did not make a decision. What he did was to allow the man on the spot to make an important political/strategic decision. The responsibility for this decision surely belonged to the president, not to MacArthur. The sooner we get away from the sanctity of the man on the spot, the better off we will be. The Goldwater-Nichols Act, by increasing the power of the unified and specified commander at the expense of the individual chiefs, is ill-conceived.

This mistaken idea that the commander on the scene has all the answers is wrong because it does not consider the critical dimensions of political strategy that the theatre commander is not in the best position to understand. This idea of making an all-knowing field commander got us into trouble with Eisenhower, regarding the decision of whether or not to take Berlin during World War II; with MacArthur in Korea; and, without question, with Westmoreland and his poorly conceived search and destroy tactic in Vietnam. The military responsibility for overall strategy must be with the chiefs—the field commander must primarily be judged on how well he executes tactically. The Goldwater-Nichols Act does just the opposite by making unified and specified commanders chiefs in political isolation. This logic will continue to be tragically wrong.

By letting us get into a position where General Westmoreland was deciding how to fight the war on the ground, the chiefs and the secretary of defense let us get into a position where, as General Palmer wrote:

> We lacked a clear objective and an attainable strategy of a decisive nature, and we relinquished the advantages of the strategic offensive to Hanoi.[68]

As included in my recommendations, an effective chairman of the Joint Chiefs, controlled and clearly responsible to the president and the secretary of defense, can help as the secretary's chief of staff. Unfortunately, under the Goldwater-Nichols Act, we run the risk of having a powerful chairman controlling what information gets to the president and the secretary of defense and thereby taking control of events. Consider what has happened to President Reagan with the Iranian situation. Vermont Royster wrote:

> But the present scandal, or whatever you wish to call it, over Iran illustrates again the necessity for a chief executive—to keep tabs on those who serve him lest they act on their own and in ways that can lead to trouble.[69]

Whether you agree that General Westmoreland faked the number of military forces in Vietnam or not, the key idea to keep in mind is how easy it is for distorted information to get to the president and the secretary of defense. Harry G. Summers, Jr., wrote:

> It remained a miracle, and in the last analysis a major failure of leadership, that during nearly three years of steadily rising combat and casualty levels, Washington did not seriously question or modify the Westmoreland strategy of attrition.[70]

Civilian leadership was responsible for the disastrous way the army was used in Vietnam. The army leadership decided to fight a search and destroy war of attrition. This was the only kind of war our army was prepared to fight. Andrew F. Krepinevich, Jr., wrote:

> The army, being denied the opportunity to win a decisive battle of annihilation by invading North Vietnam, found the attrition strategy best fit the kind of war it had prepared to fight.[71]

The army must surely be blamed for this tragic mistake, but the responsibility still remains with our civilian leadership. They should have seen that the strategy was wrong and they should have had it changed. What matters in a counterinsurgency war is protection of the population, not massive army units trying to use firepower against a highly mobile guerrilla army. This is one reason why we lost over 50,000 lives and spent 150 billion dollars in Vietnam and achieved nothing.

Vietnam was a disaster because our civilian leadership had no concept of the teamwork needed between the executive branch, Congress, the American people, and the military regarding decisions to either use or not use our armed forces. The president also did not have enough alternatives presented to him forcefully by all the chiefs and the secretary of defense working together. There is a direct relationship between alternatives considered and the quality of decisions made. Vietnam proved it.

The Goldwater-Nichols Act will insure that in the future military alternatives will be more and more limited to those of the chairman of the Joint Chiefs of Staff. This drastic change is in direct opposition to this nation's fundamental concept of civilian control of and responsibility for the effectiveness of our military forces. At best, the new system will isolate both the president and the secretary of defense. At worst, it will lead to a system that truly is based on the lowest common denominator—and eventually it can lead to military control of the country.

When President Johnson was considering not running for president in 1968 he worried about what some renegade general might do. Presidential aide Horace Busby said in a recent interview:

> He (Johnson) feared some wild general might disregard the chain of command and start his own private war with China. He was really afraid there might be some unauthorized bombing raid.[72]

America must never assume that a military takeover cannot happen in the United States. The reason it has not happened here is because, until the Goldwater-Nichols Act, the system has not allowed any nonelected military man to get into a position to control events.

Increasing the power of the JCS chairman at the expense of the other chiefs would not have helped us in Vietnam. In fact, part of the problem in Vietnam was that the president dealt primarily with Chairman Wheeler. To institutionalize this serious mistake, as the Goldwater-Nichols Act does, can lead only to trouble.

To prevent a constitutional crisis or a military disaster, the American people must become involved and understand the importance of this whole issue. Only in this way will Congress be made to understand the true meaning of what they have done by passing the Goldwater-Nichols Act. This must be done before a dangerous new momentum begins that will not help military decision making and will also create a military czar who, ultimately, can be a threat to our military effectiveness and freedom.

CHAPTER VII

CONCLUSIONS AND RECOMMENDATIONS

THE ATOMIC BOMB AND THE SPEED OF MODERN COMMUNICATION have directly and indirectly changed the relationship between the president, as civilian leader of our country, and the military establishment. We have gone from the Second World War, where:

- President Roosevelt established overall political/strategic policy but basically left the military implementation of that strategy to his military leaders, Admiral King and General Marshall. However, the president always left open to himself the option of stepping in at any level when his political strategy was at issue;
- to the Korean War, where President Truman was challenged by his field commander not only on questions of tactics but also on those of political strategy. Civilian control of the military was the clear issue here;
- to President Eisenhower, who used the atomic bomb to

establish policy and control the military. His was a military strategy based on economics;

• to the Cuban Missile Crisis, where President Kennedy not only established political policy but also was actively and thoroughly involved, as commander-in-chief, in the military implementation of that policy. He controlled events;

• to Vietnam, where President Johnson had no idea of how to be an effective president and commander-in-chief. He tried to win a war without ever having a political strategy for victory. The military made matters worse by not dealing more firmly with President Johnson. They should have told him that they could not create an effective military strategy based on his unsound political policy. Faced with not having a political strategy to work with, the army then tried to win a war essentially without a plan for doing so. Said simply, we ended up trying to fight a war of attrition. The illogic of this fact is as staggering as was the ultimate result of our efforts in Vietnam.

The new Goldwater-Nichols Defense Department Reorganization Act of 1986 is a very important piece of legislation. It will have a dramatic effect on how our military establishment is run and controlled by civilian authority. At best, it can lead to some improvement in the effectiveness and the efficiency of our military establishment. At worst, it can lead to more confusion, more bureaucracy, and ultimately, end in a constitutional crisis when the military will challenge civilian leadership and succeed. Please remember that this challenge can come in two forms. The first would be to force the president to do what the military wants on particular issues. The second would be to actually challenge the authority of civilian leaders to run the military establishment. A popular military man must never be allowed to have a position from which to gain power in the United States. The Goldwater-Nichols Act, I believe, tempts fate.

The Goldwater-Nichols Act has erred by focusing on a military solution to the problems of the Department of Defense at the expense of civilian leadership. In 1958 President Eisenhower wanted to strengthen civilian control and unity of command. He did it by greatly increasing the power and authority of the secretary of defense. President Eisenhower understood that in modern times political grand strategy had to be the basic element of military strategy formation. Somehow Senators Goldwater and Nunn took what President Eisenhower said to mean that military joint thinking and planning was the key to everything. If this were true, President Eisenhower would not have so definitely increased the power of the secretary of defense—he would have focused on the military side.

The problem we continually have is that some military leaders don't believe the secretary of defense belongs in the military chain of command because he is not a military man. He *must* be there precisely *because* he is a civilian and because one person must be in charge of the Department of Defense for the president. Unity of command must exist at the secretary's level. The secretary is the critical link between political policy, as established by the president, and military strategy formation. This makes the secretary of defense the principal person responsible for mission integration—an area where both Senator Goldwater and Senator Nunn agree we have had many problems. This vital role of mission integration most certainly cannot be executed by the military alone and surely not by the field commanders.

What the Goldwater-Nichols Act does, by giving more power to the JCS chairman, is to create another point of dangerous conflict between the secretary and the JCS chairman. The legislation adds confusion and danger to the process. No one knows how it will turn out.

As I said, many military men do not agree that the secretary of defense belongs in the military chain of command. I believe they are wrong and I also believe that this kind of thinking, unfortunately, influenced the Goldwater-Nichols Act. Why else would the legislation have focused on the JCS chairman instead of the secretary in an attempt to improve mission integration? What we must face up to is that in the modern world, the secretary of defense must be in the military chain of command because political policy is the key ingredient of effective military strategy formation, and because supervision of the military must be constant and must be the responsibility of our civilian leadership. An effective civilian leader cannot and must not try to run everything, but he must do more than simply tell the military what he wants done. He must make sure implementation is going well and, if not, recommend to the president that the policy or the people be changed.

All of these issues—and the most important issue of civilian control—have not been balanced properly in the Goldwater-Nichols Act.

Particularly in the nuclear age, civilian authority cannot stop with the creation and articulation of political goals. It can and it must include responsibility for how military strategy gets created and for ultimately approving it. The authority to develop military strategy and even tactics must be delegated to the military, but it must be done with impeccable care. Major General Jack N. Merritt wrote:

> If the army is to be used wisely, the American people should have some idea of military strategy. This is especially so since, under the Constitution, the American people through their elected representatives not only raise, support, and regulate the army but also determine the very battlefields upon which their army must fight.[1]

Our political leaders must make sure their goals are crystal clear before they give them to the military to be acted on because these objectives form the framework for the creation of military strategy and, ultimately, for what gets done tactically as well. Clausewitz wrote:

> For war is an instrument of policy; it must necessarily bear the character of policy; it must measure with policy's measure.[2]

Critics can quickly say, "Well, that's wrong—all you have to do is look at what happened with Vietnam. Was it right for the president of the United States to be personally responsible for selecting and deciding how to bomb individual targets?" The answer is no. This was, unfortunately, a case of where an insecure chief executive could not distinguish between policy formation and military implementation. He didn't understand that his responsibility was first and foremost to define our political goals and how far we would go to achieve them. He did not understand the political dimension of being commander-in-chief and neither did Secretary of Defense McNamara. No system can legislate competence. But the chiefs, strongly acting together as a unit, could have helped, and especially if they had strong support in Congress.

Putting the military in a no-win position caused these political leaders to fail because the political policy on which we established our military policy was wrong. The mistake of not having a political policy even caused the lack of effective civilian supervision that was so needed, particularly by the army, in Vietnam. If our civilian leaders knew what they were doing, we would not have fumbled into a war of attrition in Vietnam. The fact that Johnson became president after President Kennedy's death was, I believe, a cruel twist of American history.

The Cuban Missile Crisis was a better example of a president doing a much more effective job of keeping maximum civilian control over the development of political policy, military strategy, and implementation. The harmony between the political and the military was perfect. President Kennedy was able to do this because his overall political goals were clear and achievable. This enabled him to delegate military authority clearly and with precision. The military did not have to figure out what they were expected to do—the political decisions were clear. The president also was judging implementation and left nothing of a critical nature out of his presidential span of control. With the Iran/Contra affair, President Reagan has learned the devastating consequences of allowing others to use his presidential authority without keeping tight control on what they are doing.

The creators of the Goldwater-Nichols Act, although well-motivated, in my view have not understood the difference between what is a purely military, tactical matter and the role of overall political/strategic policy as established by the president. They have not understood how political policy affects strategy determination and how strategy, ultimately, determines tactics. As Clausewitz warned, "there is no such thing as a purely military strategy."[3] This applies doubly in the nuclear age.

Civilian leaders are, in the last analysis, responsible for political strategy, military strategy, and even for military implementation. They, of course, must delegate the creation of recommendations for military strategy and implementation to the military. However, it is still the responsibility of our civilian leaders to approve what the military wants to do and to hold the military accountable for implementation. That is why, under our system of government, the president's role as commander-in-chief is an active instead of a passive one.

It is important to understand that because of the atomic bomb and the speed of events, civilian authority must not only determine political policy and strategy but also be extremely involved with making sure military implementation is a direct extension of policy objectives. Said another way, our civilian leaders must always be totally responsible for overall political policy formation, but must also understand how to get policy translated into military implementation. Why? Because as so many of our presidents have found out, successful policy depends on effective execution. Policy and implementation are part of the same unit, they work together. One cannot succeed while the other fails.

Surely, the military must be responsible for tactical decisions but they must know, beyond doubt, what they are expected to do and, just as important, what they are *not* expected to do. The more we keep the military responsible only for the effectiveness of their tactical execution, the better off we will be. The Goldwater-Nichols Act moves away from this sound logic by positioning the JCS chairman as essentially the sole source of military options to the president, the secretary of defense, and the National Security Council. Eventually, so much military power, in the hands of one military man, will threaten political policy formation.

Whatever we do, we must have a system that does not blur, in any way, the responsibility of the president and the secretary of defense with any military leader. Here again, this is exactly what the new Department of Defense legislation has done. Our civilian leaders must dominate events in any crisis situation. Here is how the Senate staff's own report to the Armed Services Committee, from which much of the Goldwater-Nichols Act thinking came, put it:

> Any effort to reorganize the Department of Defense cannot diminish the authority of the president, the secretary of defense and other senior civilian authorities to control the Department of Defense. Moreover, the secretary of defense must have adequate authority to carry out his responsibilities.
>
> It is not fair to expect a civilian secretary of defense to carry all these responsibilities himself. He must be able to delegate them to subordinates who are also civilians. Any scheme must also provide protection for a weak secretary of defense who must confront strong military leadership.
>
> Any system must assure that the president and the secretary of defense are able to control detailed military operations in a crisis. Our experience of the last few years is that when military force is applied, the president and the secretary of defense have sought to control the operation with great precision. Some may question whether this is wise; none should question whether it is within their authority. Indeed, in a confrontation with the Soviet Union, such as the Cuban Missile Crisis, it is imperative that the president and the secretary be able to exercise very careful control over U.S. military forces.[4]

Many people say that the quality of advice coming from the chiefs is not good enough. Certainly, this is sometimes true and it was true in Vietnam. But the big question is why? And why would the advice get any better if it comes only from one person—the chairman? I believe the key to improving the situation lies with the secretary of defense. This person, precisely because he is involved with both political policy formulation and military strategy, must be responsible for bringing combined political/military recommendations to the president. This is why it makes sense in modern times to have the secretary of defense, as head of our military, reporting to the president. But the president must always be in complete control.

Some military leaders, such as Generals Krulak and Palmer, and Admiral Moorer, want the secretary taken out of the military chain of command. This would be sound if the secretary of defense was primarily involved with military tactics. The fact is the secretary is the responsible cabinet officer involved in the creation of the political policy that must be approved by the president. This policy must then be interpreted for the military by the secretary of defense and used as the basis for military direction and strategy formation. It is for this reason that President Eisenhower, with all his military experience, ended up getting the authority and responsibility of the secretary of defense greatly strengthened in 1953 and especially in 1958.

It is at the point of coordinating political policy with military strategy where we failed so significantly in Vietnam because McNamara did not understand the need for working with the chiefs, and unfortunately, ended up in an adversarial position with them. The primary function of the Joint Chiefs of Staff is to make the secretary as effective as possible. McNamara had no reason to create a conflicting situation between himself and his Joint Chiefs of Staff. Most probably, if the secretary and the chiefs had worked better together, they would have been in a much better position to advise and influence President Johnson when they thought he was wrong.

Admiral Moorer described Secretary McNamara's management style by testifying:

> Mr. McNamara, for instance, would sometimes get a scale model of a carrier deck and a scale model of airplanes and see whether we were telling the truth about how many you could put on a deck.[5]

Can you imagine the level of trust and teamwork this kind of behavior would create between the secretary and the chiefs?

Surely we cannot afford to create a situation where conflict drives decision making. This is what the Goldwater-Nichols Act does by blurring the role of the secretary of defense versus the JCS chairman. That is precisely what we are doing by making the chairman so powerful, initially at the expense of the other chiefs, and I strongly suspect, eventually at the expense of the secretary of defense and even the president.

For example, there is a big difference between Secretary McNamara and Secretary Weinberger. McNamara never understood that the chiefs worked for him and the president—he always had something to prove to the chiefs, Congress, and the American people. For example, when facing the decision as to what company would build the TFX or F-111, McNamara took pride in going against the advice of the Joint Chiefs. Even when right, he never understood the cost, in terms of teamwork, of being so abrasive with the chiefs. Arthur Hadley summarized:

> He believed that in systems analysis he had the answer to all problems, and that since he most perfectly understood this new faith, he was entitled to rule. He picked the General Dynamics design because unconsciously he thought by so doing he would humble the military and demonstrate his superiority by acting exactly contrary to their judgment.[6]

In contrast, Secretary Weinberger has worked well with the chiefs. He understood that he alone was responsible for the quality of advice going to the president. However, he also understood why it was in the country's best interest for the Joint Chiefs and the secretary to work together as a team with the end objective being to support the president. This attitude is why the esprit de corps has been so high in the American military during the Reagan years. I see the Goldwater-Nichols Act going against this concept of teamwork by making the JCS chairman a natural threat to both the secretary of defense and the other chiefs.

Admiral Watkins wrote:

> The lesson I draw from all this is that the quality of JCS advice is—in large degree—related to the attentiveness of and participation with the secretary of defense and the president.[7]

Vietnam was primarily a political failure—there is simply no method for building a solid military strategy on a nonexistent political base. The Goldwater-Nichols Act, by making the chairman so powerful, begins to blur the issue of keeping the military responsible for operations and tactics while being advisers only to civilian authority on issues of political policy formation. The military must also give their professional advice on whether the policy selected by our civilian leaders can be militarily implemented.

In fact, I agree strongly with Admiral King who totally opposed the idea of one military man dominating our military establishment. His views were summarized in *The New York Times:*

> Admiral King attacked the army's proposal for a unified department in which there will be a chief of staff of all the armed forces as an infringement on the prerogatives of the president of the United States as commander-in-chief of the armed forces.[8]

The point of ultimate unification must be with the president alone. No civilian or military man must ever be placed in a position to challenge presidential authority, and this surely includes the secretary of defense and the JCS chairman. One mistake in this direction is making the chairman of the Joint Chiefs the all-knowing, number one military man in this country. The other point to consider is how powerful the secretary of defense should be. The more our military leaders work together directly with the president, the better.

The Goldwater-Nichols Act implies that all of the mistakes

of our recent past were military. I don't agree. For example, in Vietnam we had such great problems because the secretary of defense had poor judgment when it came to political issues and clearly did not know how to work with the military. He kept trying to prove that he knew more than they did on everything, especially on certain types of tactical matters, and this resulted in McNamara running over the chiefs but accomplishing nothing. Strangely, on other issues, like the ill-conceived search and destroy tactic of the army, both President Johnson and Secretary McNamara did not act when it was their responsibility to do so. In addition, the fact that the chiefs were advisers and not in the chain of command did not help their effectiveness. General Palmer:

> Those who frequently blame the JCS for much of what seems to be wrong in the Department of Defense should bear in mind that the chiefs can only advise their civilian superiors on the strategic implications of the international scene and make recommendations as to the kind of defense establishment needed to protect U.S. interests. . . . Thus, strategic and political guidance, as well as fiscal guidance, must of necessity emanate from the civilian leadership, that is, the secretary of defense and the president.[9]

The country might also have been much better off if President Johnson had been seeing, on a regular basis, *all* of the chiefs instead of just JCS Chairman Wheeler. The Goldwater-Nichols Act runs the distinct risk of making this fundamental mistake an established procedure. General Ridgway wrote:

> There is no one human being who knows enough of the detailed conduct of military operations on land, sea, and in the air to be competent to advise the civil authorities on all three.[10]

The key factor, I believe, is to have clear-cut harmony between the president, his secretary of defense, the chiefs, and Congress. How to best accomplish this is not covered by the

Goldwater-Nichols Act. The core of our military problem of getting the people's support to fight a war to defend our vital interests has not been improved. This vacuum leaves the public, even today, in a very insecure position. The debate over the ill-conceived War Powers Act makes this point crystal clear.

All future presidents, I believe, should be very careful about where they get their advice. A president can be blind-sided by the secretary of defense and surely by the chairman of the Joint Chiefs. That is why the president must make sure he or she can clearly separate the recommendation of the secretary of defense from those of the chairman and from those of the individual chiefs.

In his book, *A Journey Amongst the Good and the Great,* Andy Kerr writes:

> Yet, we concluded, interservice rivalry is not per se a bad thing. There can be important benefits from the competition of ideas. Only when out of control is it harmful. Properly channeled and controlled, it would merely result in alternatives being offered to a decision maker.
>
> The decision maker, we argued, should not be a single chief of staff. Because of his background and experience, the single chief would tend to favor the military philosophy of his own service. A dangerously one-sided national strategy could result. Also, civilian control of the military would be endangered by the very fact that the military would indeed speak with a single voice: Congress and the Executive would not have the opportunity to weigh and evaluate competing proposals. At the end of this spectrum is the danger of the emergence of a man on horseback.[11]

As President Kennedy learned, negatively, as a result of the Bay of Pigs failure and, positively, during the Cuban Missile Crisis, the creation of options is the key to effective decision making. Most important, *who* is making the recommendations and *why* must be scrutinized closely by any president. The president is and must always be the sole decision maker and, thereby, can never allow any civilian or military expert to overwhelm him or dominate his involvement in decision making.

Bruce Palmer wrote:

> In our system of government, the president, with his dual role as civilian chief executive and commander-in-chief of the armed forces, is the indispensable key to national security. For the president to control the nation's armed forces, he must command them; he cannot delegate this to his secretary of defense or to the military chiefs. He must have direct access to the Joint Chiefs of Staff, collectively and individually, and must regularly see them. If he shunts them off or allows his secretary of defense to isolate the chiefs, he does so at the nation's peril. The president is the commander-in-chief and there is no substitute for his forceful and visible leadership in discharging this supreme command function over the Department of Defense and the armed forces.[12]

Making the chairman the most powerful military leader in our history can cause very serious problems. It can:

- Limit the information and alternative points of view going to the president and the secretary of defense, thereby resulting in the military becoming, in time, more powerful than the president and secretary of defense. Surely, we would never want the military competing with civilian authority for power. Why would we ever want to risk possibly our most important freedom—civilian control of the military and, in time, quite possibly our entire way of life?
- Change the balance within the Joint Chiefs; whereby, within the military, there will be no effective checks and balances on the JCS chairman.
- Result in the ten worldwide commanders essentially reporting to the chairman. What could be more risky, because in time all military power will be solidified in the chairman?
- Result in the chairman being the only military person involved in policy, strategy, and implementation. Nothing

could be more dangerous not only from the viewpoint of civilian control of the military but also from the creation of alternative points of view for consideration by the president and the secretary of defense.

As former Chief of Naval Operations Admiral James D. Watkins testified in 1985:

> Unitary advice offered by a single military individual, no matter how competent, with a single service background and a single point of view, will not ensure the quality and objectivity of civilian control that a democracy demands.[13]

In summary, the Goldwater-Nichols Act of 1986 can, under the best of circumstances, result in greater efficiency for our military establishment—but we must ask at what expense. *The losers are both civilian control of the military and the effectiveness by which the civilian and military leaders work together in the delicate process of going from political policy through strategy to military implementation.*

John W. Spanier wrote:

> Since it is not customary for an administration to issue specific orders to a military executive thousands of miles away, the latter can, owing to poor judgment or deliberate design, make decisions whose political and strategic consequences may well prevent the achievement of the government's objectives, if not undermine them. Necessity may, therefore, compel a re-examination of the tradition of military freedom lest it excuse us into disaster. In limited warfare not only military strategy, but on occasions even military tactics, have important political repercussions.[14]

The idea of having one all-knowing chairman of the Joint Chiefs of Staff backed up by a powerful vice chairman running things is a dangerous illusion. Its illogic is heightened by believing that in the name of efficiency it makes sense to increase the power of the ten combatant commanders around the world to the advantage of the chairman and at the expense of the other chiefs. This change is further flawed because it will prove to be accomplished at the expense of overall policy formation and civilian control. Limiting alternatives considered, by downgrading all the service chiefs and all the service secretaries, *will prove to be a colossal error of the Goldwater-Nichols Act.*

General Ridgway wrote:

> The departments of the army, navy, and the air force should retain their separate identities; their traditions and pride of service should be zealously preserved; and the civilian heads of these departments and the senior uniformed subordinate of each, should all have equal opportunity for the expression of their views before the highest executive and legislative councils of the nation, with ready access, insured, if necessary *by legislative prescription,* to such councils at any time that, in their conscientious judgments, the importance of a problem demands a hearing.
>
> It is highly undesirable to have the chairman of the Joint Chiefs of Staff vested with command authority over the other members thereof.[15]

As difficult as it is for us to understand and live with, the control of our civilian authority cannot be ambiguous. *The days of sending a General Pershing over to fight a war are over. The supremacy of the field commander must be ended.* The Goldwater-Nichols Act brings it back and makes it worse because of the support a powerful chairman can give any field commander. Consider what might have happened in Korea if an all-powerful military leader in Washington had supported General MacArthur.

As former Secretary of the Navy John F. Lehman put it:

> Most important, the inability of civilian leaders to compete with the view of a single, all-powerful senior officer

would leave a president no choice but to disregard completely or accept without question the opinion of his sole military adviser. The result would be to inhibit civilian authorities from directing national defense.[16]

Recommendations

The Goldwater-Nichols Act will not improve the management of our military establishment. The law must be changed. Our choice is to wait for mistakes to be made under this new legislation or face facts and change the law before the country suffers.

The Presidential Blue Ribbon Commission on Defense Management (Packard Commission) made recommendations, some of which were included in the Goldwater-Nichols Act. My first recommendation is for the president to follow up the work of the Packard Commission by appointing a special commission to analyze the strengths and weaknesses of the Goldwater-Nichols Act. To head the commission, I am recommending former Chairman of the Joint Chiefs of Staff General John W. Vessey, Jr.

Based on the research and analysis I have done, I firmly believe we need a more logical way for managing our military establishment. My specific recommendations are as follows:

Recommendation Number One: *Have the chairman designated as the military chief of staff to the secretary of defense in addition to his role as JCS chairman.* In this way the chairman would never be in a position of competing with the secretary of defense but would be a source of alternatives beyond what the service chiefs might create. It also would be logical to expect that the chairman's alternatives would be particularly sensitive to political policy as established by the president. With a chairman gaining all of his authority from the president and the secretary of defense, we actually have helped to insure civilian control of the military and the overall effectiveness of the secretary of defense and our military fighting forces.

As chief of staff to the secretary of defense, the chairman will now be properly controlled and in the right position to understand and coordinate decision making between the president, the secretary of defense, and the chiefs. As chief of staff to the secretary, the chairman can indeed help the secretary and the Joint Chiefs coordinate joint military operations. Only with the chairman positioned as chief of staff to the secretary would I recommend that military orders be sent out by the service chiefs most concerned and by the chairman representing the secretary of defense. Once policy and strategy have been decided, it makes sense to coordinate orders going to the unified and specified commanders around the world. This system would apply in both peacetime and wartime.

The chairman would still have much access to the president at the National Security Council meetings and at the regular meetings between all the chiefs, the secretary of defense, and the president.

The president must continue to pick the JCS chairman; however, a change must be made whereby this happens regularly and early, in any new administration. The president needs and must expect a close relationship between his secretary of defense and the JCS chairman. The Goldwater-Nichols Act continues to allow the present JCS chairman to remain when a new administration begins. This can be a very serious problem that is best solved by enabling the president to more easily either keep the man in office at the time or by letting the president pick the person he wants. Critics might say this makes the JCS chairman more political. However, the benefit of the president having a JCS chairman he or she can trust far outweighs any possible political negative.

It is very significant to make the JCS chairman also chief of staff to the secretary of defense. It is an effective way to increase the military options available to the secretary and improves his ability to make sound military decisions based on solid and informed military advice. A structure where the secretary is directly supported by civilian deputy secretaries of defense for each service, the individual service chiefs, and the JCS chairman, as his chief of staff, is the best way to increase the effectiveness of joint military operations. In this way coordinated political strategic direction would come from leaders in Washington to theatre commanders for their implementation. This makes a very clear demarcation between policy formation and implementation which becomes, as it should be, the field commanders' primary responsibility.

One of the controversial aspects of the Goldwater-Nichols Act is having the unified and specified commanders from all branches of the services essentially reporting to the all-powerful chairman of the Joint Chiefs. Whether this is an improvement or not will have to be studied after this legislation has had time to be tested.

My thought is for the chiefs of all the services to be back in the chain of command and made heads of their services as, logically, most Americans believe they are now. The overall system then becomes stronger and more logical by designating the JCS chairman as military chief of staff to the secretary of defense.

The Goldwater-Nichols Act makes the secretary of defense and the JCS chairman adversaries. Making the JCS chairman chief of staff to the secretary makes them what they must be: natural allies.

Recommendation Number Two: *Put the individual service chiefs back in the military chain of command as was the case during World War II.*

This important change would make the nation's leading military officers leaders again instead of just advisers as they are now. This change would also prevent the chiefs from being further downgraded as is the case under the Goldwater-Nichols Act. The problem with the chiefs is that they are not, in fact, clearly heads of anything. They cannot be heads of anything as advisers when the unified and specified commanders have the command authority. The facts are the chief of naval operations can't move a ship nor can the army chief of staff move a division. *The source of all our recent major military problems comes from the fact that the chiefs are not totally responsible for what happens.* This contrasts sharply with the situation that existed with Admiral King and General Marshall being heads of their services in every sense of the word during World War II.

Lawrence Korb summarized:

> Legally the JCS have been removed from the operational realm and have been reduced to the status of a planning agency and an advisory group.[17]

Senator Goldwater was right in his October 4, 1985, Senate speech saying, "Without effective mission integration unification of the four services means nothing." However, effective mission integration begins with having four strong individual services, each headed by one officer. The secretary of defense, using the individual chiefs, the JCS chairman, and the civilian heads of the services, is responsible for accomplishing mission integration. The mistake of having downgraded the chiefs so drastically since World War II cannot be corrected by increasing the power of the JCS chairman. One military man in charge during World War II would have been a bad idea.

To make things worse, what the Goldwater-Nichols Act has done is to make the chiefs even less important, with their roles limited more and more to issues such as training and supply. Clearly, this new reality will make them less effective and less important regarding strategy and execution. Considering his strong role in getting the Goldwater-Nichols Act passed, I was surprised when Congressman Les Aspin said:

> I'm wondering what's happening to the chiefs. They're not the players they once were.[18]

General Bruce Palmer, Jr., agrees that the chiefs should be placed in the chain of command. He wrote:

> Moreover, present statutes should be revised so that the JCS are formally placed in the chain rather than continued in their present off-line advisory position.[19]

The chiefs have had a great deal of prestige, particularly based on the key role the Joint Chiefs had during World War II, but no real final responsibility for the total running of the military portion of the Department of Defense. We must centralize military strategic decision making and responsibility with the chiefs, while decentralizing only execution of what the chiefs have ordered—on command from the secretary of defense and the president—to the unified and specified commanders around the world.

The facts are that when a field commander is doing a good job, he should have all the authority needed to get the job done. But a field commander must have a military boss in Washington who is sensitive to precisely what the president and the secretary of defense want accomplished politically. General Eisenhower in Europe and Admiral Nimitz in the Pacific could never have been successful without clear direction from a single military leader in Washington. Regarding Vietnam, the nation would have done well to have General Westmoreland closely supervised by the army chief of staff. This same logic applied to General MacArthur in Korea.

Therefore, many of our military problems since World War II have resulted from the chiefs being advisers or managers instead of leaders in the chain of command with unquestioned authority to act. John L. Frisbee wrote:

> Throughout the post-World War II years, the Joint Chiefs of Staff organization has been little understood by the general public; frequently criticized for performing as the Congress intended it to perform (i.e., as an advisory committee concerned with the military factors of national security policy); often blamed for decisions over which it had little or no control; and seldom praised for the genuine contributions it has made to the management of defense affairs.[20]

It is very difficult for any adviser to get anything accomplished. This is particularly true in a military organization. In fact, reading the testimony of the chiefs before Congress convinces me that even they have become confused on the important distinction between being an adviser or manager versus a leader. This situation is further confused by the fact that the president quite logically still considers the chiefs responsible for military strategy formation and implementation. Why? Because it makes sense for him to think this way. They are supposed to be heads of their services and members of the Joint Chiefs of Staff. Why should they not be answerable to the president and the secretary of defense as heads of their individual services and responsible for unifying overall strategy?

The place where political policy merges with military strategy formation must be in Washington with the secretary of defense and the president. This process must also include joint mission integration. It is at this point where the secretary must use the JCS chairman and the other individual service heads to give their very best recommendations. However, it must always be crystal clear that the responsibility for mission integration belongs to the secretary and the president no matter what the military has to say. Political policy and unity of command must be achieved at the secretary's level before presentation to the president. A diversion to either the secretary of defense or the JCS chairman is wrong.

After political and military strategy have been defined, it must be up to the individual chief in Washington to give the orders to the CINCs. The unified and specified commanders cannot and must not be on top of the military chain of command. It is what we have now. It is wrong. It must be understood as a serious problem and changed.

Unfortunately, the Goldwater-Nichols Act has assumed incorrectly that the field commander must be free to run the show on his own. This situation can never be right because critical elements like political policy must come from the president and the secretary of defense while the chiefs must be responsible, first, for running their services worldwide and, second, for helping to coordinate all joint military operations with the active leadership of the secretary of defense and the president.

Field commanders do not have the time, perspective, or authority to make joint operations effective on their own. The more we keep field commanders responsible for implementation, the better off we will be. The Goldwater-Nichols Act has not focused on this fundamental organization problem. All it has done is to move power to the JCS chairman. From every viewpoint, this will not solve the basic problem of a mission integration outlined by Senators Goldwater and Nunn, but will create new ones.

Based on clear and, when needed, forceful direction from Washington, the area commander can then determine the military strategy he will use and the corresponding tactics. Even here the chiefs must be responsible for making sure the area commander is right. Only then can tactics become the responsibility of the unified and specified commanders. We have had poor military execution because clear direction and responsibility from the top have been missing. Lack of effective control from the top caused failures in Korea, Vietnam, Beirut, and the Iranian rescue mission. A misunderstanding of what the chiefs must be responsible for versus the theatre commanders has gotten us into many problems and will continue to do so under the Goldwater-Nichols Act.

Consider this astounding contradiction: In our system, not one of our most experienced, best qualified senior officers of any of our services has command authority over his fighting forces. This authority is vested in the ten unified and specified commanders around the world. The quality of the orders coming from Washington is therefore weak and fuzzy because the authority of the chiefs is weak and fuzzy. The problem of the chiefs has been undermanagement of military operations, not overmanagement, while the administrative staffs of the chiefs in Washington have been increasing at the expense of their command responsibility.

During World War II we were handicapped with the belief that the theatre commanders were all-knowing. Fortunately, this situation was balanced by the fact that the heads of the army and navy, General Marshall and Admiral King, were both members of the Joint Chiefs and clear heads of their services. They were heads of their services because they were in the chain of command reporting to the president. They—not the theatre commanders—were responsible to the president for how effectively political policy got translated into military strategy and how effectively it was implemented. Because the atomic age makes political policy more critical, the point of primary responsibility for moving from political policy to military strategy is now more than ever the responsibility of the president.

What the Goldwater-Nichols Act implies is that in peacetime the secretary of defense should be in charge of the Department of Defense, but in wartime more power must switch to the JCS chairman. This kind of unclear reasoning is a big part of our problem. Political policy must always be the key ingredient of military decision making and that is why, in 1958, President Eisenhower insisted on increasing the power of the secretary of defense. He understood that because of nuclear power and modern communication, the role of the secretary must grow.

In his April 3, 1958, message to Congress, President Eisenhower said:

> The authority of the secretary of defense will be clarified to enable him to function as a fully effective agent of the president as commander-in-chief.[21]

In addition, there is just no efficient or effective method for the worldwide commanders to be as sensitive and as knowledgeable about political policy as they would need to be in peacetime and, particularly, in wartime. It should not and can not be their responsibility. Ten powerful officers away from Washington are not in a position to interpret political policy nor can they be responsible for uniting their individual efforts. The initial joint strategic thinking leading to the creation of military strategy must be done in Washington. Can you imagine what would have happened in World War II if the unquestioned heads of the services responsible for military strategy were not Chief of Naval Operations Fleet Admiral Ernest J. King and Army Chief of Staff General of the Army George C. Marshall?

It might be interesting to consider what would have happened in World War II if we had the Goldwater-Nichols Act and if General Marshall was JCS chairman. This reality could very well have prevented the president from hearing Admiral King's views firsthand not only on naval strategy but also on overall worldwide strategy as well. The president had the great benefit of hearing alternatives from Marshall and King; General Arnold, for the Army Air Corps (when appropriate), and Admiral Leahy, the JCS chairman. In fact, after the war, the air force was separated from the army precisely because army operations and air operations were so different. Without thinking it through, under the Goldwater-Nichols Act, it sounds right to put total emphasis on joint air, ground, and naval operations. However, to assume that joint operations are the key to everything ignores the fact that joint operations depend foremost on strong air, ground, and naval capability.

We were lucky during World War II that King and Marshall did such an effective job of balancing their authority as heads of their services versus the sometimes overly powerful role of the theatre commanders. King and Marshall knew when to push their commanders, like General Eisenhower and Admiral Nimitz. But the important point is that they could and did *order,* not request, these commanders to do what political policy dictated had to be done. In retrospect, it is clear that the dominant role of King and Marshall was far more important than having theatre commanders running the show on their own. If the theatre commanders would have functioned on their own it would have been a disorganized effort. Jointness must happen initially at the civilian level, with the president and the secretary of defense coordinating with the individual service chiefs. The Goldwater-Nichols Act fights this critical need.

President Roosevelt was very smart to have Admiral King and General Marshall as the clear heads of their services and, ultimately, responsible for what got done. To move from political policy to strategy formation to implementation, all President Roosevelt had to do was communicate with King and Marshall. The same logic applied if things did not go well—King and Marshall were responsible, not the theatre commanders.

Roosevelt knew that poor implementation could destroy the

effectiveness of any good political policy idea, and that is why he made King and Marshall so strong but always subject to his authority as commander-in-chief. Often Roosevelt signed notes to King and Marshall as "FDR Commander-in-Chief." I'm sure they knew why.

What the president and the secretary of defense need most are alternative ways to solve military problems even if these recommendations are initially in conflict. That is why conflict within the Joint Chiefs is good, not bad, and should be encouraged. Effective policy formation is always improved by the development of alternate viewpoints, particularly when we are dealing with such complicated issues as ground, air, and naval warfare. Admiral Watkins put it well when he said:

> This chairman of the Joint Chiefs (Vessey) gave a presentation before the National Security Council that was reported to have been one of the finest presentations ever made over there by a chairman of the Joint Chiefs of Staff, because he put in the dissenting opinion of every member explaining why we dissented and our rationale. . . . The President will be better served by five people voting 3-to-2 than one person with an assured yes vote.[22]

The consequences of decreasing even further the power and command function of the service chiefs is a major error of the new legislation. My recommendation is to do just the opposite: Put the chiefs back in the chain of command as the unquestioned heads of their services.

Recommendation Number Three: *Have the service chiefs and their individual staffs become the military staff of the secretary of defense. On the civilian side I would have the individual service secretaries and their staff become the military staff of the secretary of defense.* This way the secretary of defense would have both the military and civilian parts of the military establishment reporting directly to him with no fuzziness as is the case now. I would also recommend changing the titles of the service secretaries to deputy secretaries of defense for either ground, air, or navy. The service deputy secretaries would then work closely with the secretary of defense on all issues, including strategy and mission integration. They would become his key civilian staff. On the military side the individual chiefs would also be helping the secretary on strategy and mission integration. This system would have the deputy secretaries of defense and the military service chiefs as equals. The point is to make them sources of alternatives for the secretary of defense. Under this system both the deputy secretaries and the service chiefs gain in authority and in value to the secretary of defense and ultimately the President. The point of integration would come at the secretary of defense's level. Thus, the major function of the secretary of defense becomes worldwide military strategy formation and mission integration.

Senator Nunn said in his October 4, 1985, Senate speech, "No one in DoD has responsibility for the mission as an output." Streamlining and simplifying the organizational structure of the Office of the Secretary of Defense is to increase the effectiveness of the secretary of defense by highlighting the fact that his most important function is worldwide military strategy formation and mission integration.

This organizational change would be the most sensible and direct way to increase the overall responsibility and effectiveness of the secretary as head of the Department of Defense. It would insure effective civilian control and the total involvement of the secretary in both peacetime and wartime. Simplification of the reporting system will also help overall teamwork by directly coordinating the efforts of the chiefs and the deputy secretaries of defense. General Vessey testified:

> One of the things that we learned in our review is that the objective of the exercise should be to make the key man in the defense organization as effective as he can be. That key man is the secretary of defense.[23]

To follow General Vessey's thoughts, a single point of coordination is needed. The Goldwater-Nichols Act blurs the issue by establishing two points of coordination and authority; one with the JCS chairman, which I believe is, at best, inefficient and, at worst, potentially a threat to civilian control of the military. The other point of coordination and authority is with the secretary of defense.

What we need is one clear point of authority: the secretary of defense, directly supported by two key staffs—one, civilian; the other, military. The capability of the secretary's staff would automatically increase and they would be uniquely qualified to help him run a more united Defense Department. A further refinement would also be needed to reduce the number of people reporting directly to the secretary of defense.

Another obvious benefit would be a reduction in the bureaucracy. For example, there would no longer be a need for the Office of the Secretary of Defense to duplicate much of the capability now existing in the service and civilian staffs of the Joint Chiefs and the service secretaries.

Under the Goldwater-Nichols Act, greater inefficiency will become a reality as the JCS chairman and the vice chairman add staffs that duplicate the staffs of the Joint Chiefs, the service secretaries, and the staff of the secretary of defense.

This simplified system, which balances the civilian with the military side, will enable the secretary of defense to have a variety of options and recommendations coming to him in a way that will increase his flexibility. Through this simplified system he will be able to have greater effective control than has been the case. This will enable him to focus on grand strategy, mission integration, and to thereby make the most effective recommendations to the president. Once presidential approval has been received, orders will go out to the unified and specified commanders from the secretary of defense through the specific chief the secretary designates as executive agent for the Joint Chiefs. To insure that the orders are coordinated and what the secretary wants, I would have all orders signed by the JCS chairman serving as agent for the secretary of defense. This system, with its checks and balances, will finally place the secretary on top of the Department of Defense and, therefore, in the best position to focus on grand strategy and mission integration.

Recommendation Number Four: *To pass a law that forces the president to meet regularly with all the Joint Chiefs of Staff.* There is no better way to keep *everybody* informed and to make certain both majority and minority views are all considered. Often what the majority recommends is not good enough. Clearly, this has been a problem with the Joint Chiefs, which can best be solved by making it mandatory for any president to meet regularly with the secretary of defense and all the chiefs.

Former Chairman Thomas H. Moorer:

> I don't think any president has had enough discussions with the Joint Chiefs of Staff. I really don't. He sees the Chairman all the time, but he doesn't see the other members.[24]

No president can afford to become isolated from the Joint Chiefs of Staff as a body. The only way this would make sense is for the chiefs to be so downgraded in the command structure that their advice and capability become meaningless. This is precisely what the Goldwater-Nichols Act begins to do by increasing the JCS chairman's power and the CINCs at the expense of the service chiefs.

The logic for this is that joint operations must dominate all thinking. I believe the reverse. You must have strong individual services first before you can begin the process of coordination. The individual chiefs must be the key to both individual service effectiveness and the effectiveness of joint operations. Under the new law the chairman will be in a position to push the chiefs more and more out of joint involvement. In his testimony before Congress, Air Force Chief of Staff Charles A. Gabriel said, "I think taking the chiefs out of the joint business will be a big mistake."[25]

The Goldwater-Nichols Act enables the JCS chairman to dominate the advice going to our civilian leaders. Only he will see the president, the secretary of defense, and the National Security Council. This is the formula for poor decision making, military dominance, or both. As General Palmer said:

It is dangerous to submerge divergent views on important issues and a disservice to civilian authority.[26]

A president must always be on guard against a dominant or not fully qualified secretary of defense. We surely don't, for example, want any secretary of defense to consider himself commander-in-chief. The president must be, in every sense of the word, our only commander-in-chief. To keep all options open and to make clear who is on top of the chain of command, all presidents must meet regularly with the secretary of defense, the JCS chairman, and the other chiefs. This new process must be made law. (If a law is too strong or unconstitutional, at least let us get the tradition going with a resolution passed by both Houses of the Congress.)

Recommendation Number Five: *I recommend that congressional leaders attend specific National Security Council meetings that specifically involve decisions concerning the possible use of American military forces.* We can no longer allow the executive branch to act without congressional involvement. The Constitution gave Congress the right to declare war for good reasons. Therefore, the War Powers Act, which enables the president to use military force for sixty days without congressional approval, must be replaced by congressional leaders attending National Security Council meetings when the issue of using force is discussed.

I am aware of the constitutional problem of having the Congress involved in meetings of the National Security Council. Hopefully, this issue can be avoided by having the congressional leaders meet with the National Security Council only when the issue of using our military forces is discussed. Even then the reason for their being at the meetings would be solely to hear what the executive branch is considering and to give their opinions regarding how Congress will react. U.S. military force must never be used without the president and Congress working together. This relationship is essential in the modern world, when a mistake made in the field can have such drastic consequences for our country. Only in the case of a dreadful emergency like a nuclear attack can the president be allowed to act on his own.

J. Brian Atwood, who helped to draft the War Powers Act in 1974, understands the clear need to get the president and Congress to work more closely together. His idea:

> What is needed is a special "leadership committee" that would regularly consult with the executive branch on the world's hot spots—a committee made up of the leaders of both houses and the chairman and ranking members of the foreign affairs, armed services and intelligence committees. Such a committee would wield clout and credibility that none of these leaders or committees could possibly muster standing alone.[27]

Although he understands the problem, I don't happen to agree with Mr. Atwood on this recommendation or, for that matter, on the War Powers Act. This act does absolutely nothing to help the president and Congress work together. My idea of having congressional leaders attend NSC meetings, I believe, makes more sense.

Recent events in Afghanistan have proved how effective the policy of the United States can be in a most difficult situation when the executive branch and the Congress work together. It was agreed to supply arms and other material to the Afghans because this would keep the pressure on the Soviets. In the case of Nicaragua, an effective policy has not been developed because Congress has consistently disagreed with the executive branch.

Even one of the key military supporters of the Goldwater-Nichols Act, Army Chief of Staff General Edward C. Meyer, agrees that the military must meet frequently not only with the executive branch but also with Congress as well. General Meyer:

> The key to this system [JCS during World War II] was frequent access by the military to the decision-making bodies of government, both executive and legislative.[28]

I don't believe President Johnson could have used combat troops so easily in Vietnam or gotten the Tonkin Gulf Resolution passed had the leadership of Congress been present at NSC meetings where these issues were discussed. Whatever we can do to force the president and Congress to work together will greatly benefit our country. To me "no more Vietnam" means "no more presidential wars."

I would have eight members of Congress at the meetings: The speaker of the House, the Senate majority leader, the House and Senate minority leaders, the chairman of the House and Senate Armed Services Committee, plus the minority members of each committee. This would at least be the beginning of finding ways for some group to speak for Congress. There is no question that Congress must speak as a body on crucial issues involving national security.

This system will return us to the checks and balances the Constitution gave us by making the president commander-in-chief while only Congress can declare war. The United States can never fight a war without the total support of the people. Vietnam surely taught us this lesson.

Recommendation Number Six: *When a military subject is being discussed, have all the chiefs meet with the National Security Council, not just the chairman and the vice chairman.* This is the best way to insure that all options are considered and evaluated. No one military man can understand or effectively communicate divergent viewpoints. It will also be the best way to make sure all civilian and military leaders are kept totally informed.

How can it possibly make sense to have only the JCS chairman or the vice chairman attend the National Security Council meetings? They are not all-knowing on military matters, so all they can do is limit alternatives considered and isolate our other key military leaders. As General Vessey testified:

> This particular body here [the Joint Chiefs] has taken the view the president is going to get our advice whether he asks for it or not, and I think that is the right thing, the right view for the Joint Chiefs of Staff to have. . . .

> He doesn't have to take it, certainly, but we need to understand that he needs our advice and we need to get it to him on time on the important national security issues.[29]

This broader system could have helped us make better decisions concerning Vietnam. It could prevent another such disaster. In 1954 we were fortunate that General Ridgway could get to President Eisenhower. If he could have attended National Security Council meetings, he would have had a proper place to outline his views without fear of the JCS chairman.

Whether all the chiefs or a specific chief should attend specific National Security Council meetings should be decided by the president and the secretary of defense, depending on what is being discussed.

Recommendation Number Seven: *Have the vice chairman report directly to the JCS chairman and assist him in any way the chairman directs.* The vice chairman absolutely should not be the number two man in the military and surely should not outrank the service chiefs. The last thing we would want is for the chairman and the vice chairman to dominate military thinking as they will under the Goldwater-Nichols Act.

Interestingly enough, the Packard Blue Ribbon Presidential Commission on Defense Management never even conceived of the vice chairman as being made superior to the other chiefs. The final report said:

> The vice chairman should assist the chairman by representing the interests of the CINCs . . . and performing such other duties as the chairman may prescribe.[30]

Having the vice chairman work clearly with the CINCs and the director of the Joint Chiefs could be a good idea. This may be an effective way to help joint military operations.

The Joint Chiefs themselves voted against having a vice chairman. Since this officer is not a member of the Joint Chiefs, they sensibly referred to him as deputy chairman. General Vessey:

> Now let's sit down and write the duties of the deputy chairman, recognizing what the duties of the JCS are under law in relationship with the commanders-in-chief of the unified and specified commands and with the secretary of defense and the president. We agreed we would try to write the duties of the deputy chairman, and where he sits in this hierarchy of things, and what he is to do.
>
> Well, as a body we all tried to do that and we couldn't come up with satisfactory answers. As a result, we concluded that we were better off without a deputy chairman.[31]

To complicate matters, under the new legislation the vice chairman is the number two man in the military and not a member of the Joint Chiefs of Staff. The meaning is clear: The JCS chairman and the vice chairman will, over time, run the show. This includes building another vast bureaucracy.

Admiral Moorer:

> Again, you know the way we try to solve problems is always to add some more people. The minute you get a vice chief, he has to have a staff himself, and four or five officers, and the thing gets bigger and bigger. . . .
>
> I think it is totally unnecessary. If I could be reincarnated and start over as chairman and they gave me a vice chairman, I would tell him to go home.[32]

The Goldwater-Nichols Act makes the vice chairman the second-highest-ranking military officer in our military. This is a fact even though he is not a member of the Joint Chiefs of Staff. The last thing a reorganization of the Joint Chiefs needs is another costly bureaucracy duplicating and competing with the Office of the Secretary of Defense, the service secretaries, and the Joint Chiefs.

Let's get the vice chairman placed where he belongs—assisting the JCS chairman without vast powers that make no sense. This will be the best way to improve overall military decision making.

Summary of Recommendations

These recommendations would position the secretary of defense on top of the Department of Defense, with both a military staff headed by the individual service chiefs and a civilian staff headed by the civilian deputy secretaries of defense reporting to him. This is the most efficient and effective way to manage the Department of Defense. Civilian control and military effectiveness would benefit greatly. In addition, the Office of the Secretary of Defense no longer would be duplicating the work of the individual service staffs or the civilian service staffs. The Department of Defense would finally be properly structured for peacetime and wartime decision making.

The chiefs would be back in the chain of command as leaders. They would be totally responsible for the effectiveness of their individual services. This logic would recognize the fact that effective joint operations depend first on having superbly qualified individual services, not the other way around—which is the focus of the Goldwater-Nichols Act.

Regarding orders going to the ten war-fighting commanders, these will be sent by the chief who, in the secretary of defense's opinion, is best qualified and will be held responsible for what happens, while a chairman would always be involved as agent for the secretary of defense. It is logical for the commander of the Pacific to receive his orders from the chief of naval operations and for the commander in Europe to get his from the army chief of staff. However, the secretary must always have the flexibility to make changes based on the situation. For example, it would have been more logical to have the commandant of the Marine Corps in charge of our Beirut forces instead of the Supreme Allied Commander Europe.

As chief of staff to the secretary, the JCS chairman now would be in a perfect position to directly support the secretary, particularly on issues involving joint military operations. He becomes a source of ideas over and above both the chiefs and the deputy secretaries of defense and another set of eyes and ears for the secretary. *The chairman's and the secretary's focus must always be the same.* The chairman does not become a bureaucracy unto himself. He will get his authority and responsibility from the president and the secretary. This does everything possible to insure civilian control, overall flexibility, and overall effectiveness.

This new system would insure civilian control and improve overall effectiveness by making the points of responsibility crystal clear.

- The secretary would have an efficient, simplified system with the chiefs reporting to him on the military side and the deputy secretaries of defense reporting on the civilian side.
- The Joint Chiefs would be made leaders in the chain of command, not advisers or managers.
- The deputy secretaries of defense would be more properly positioned versus the service chiefs and the JCS chairman.
- The focus of the JCS chairman would be to directly support all efforts of the secretary of defense and the president in both peacetime and wartime.
- There will be less bureaucracy, not more, as will be the case under the Goldwater-Nichols Act.

Everything will be more effective if it is clearly understood that political policy formation is the exclusive responsibility of our civilian leaders, while they must also be involved in approving and supervising military strategy and even implementation to varying degrees, depending on the situation. General Maxwell Taylor wrote: ". . . the JCS advise; they cannot decide these matters [political issues]. Decision is the responsibility of civilian leadership."[33]

The chiefs, because of their position relative to the president and the secretary of defense, would, as Admiral King and General Marshall did during World War II, be the key players in translating political policy into military implementation for the ten combatant commanders. Getting the ten area commanders totally involved in budgets and the translation of policy into implementation is illogical and dangerous, as we found out with MacArthur in Korea.

The relationship between President Roosevelt and his chiefs of staff worked well during World War II because the chiefs knew precisely what Roosevelt wanted accomplished and they had the authority to get things done. Admiral King was head of the navy and Marine Corps, General Marshall was head of the army, and—subject to General Marshall—General Arnold was head of the Army Air Corps. There was no question about this fact while Admiral Leahy, as chief of staff to the president and JCS chairman, served the useful purpose of bringing a different point of view to the president when needed.

Under the system which I believe is best, the chairman of the Joint Chiefs would have the precise amount of authority the president and the secretary of defense want him to have, not one ounce more. This way the chiefs and the chairman would balance against each other for the benefit of our civilian leaders, instead of having the JCS chairman and the secretary of defense in competition, as may very well be the result of the Goldwater-Nichols Act. In addition, defining the chairman as chief of staff and deputy to the secretary of defense and possibly to the president will serve the added purpose of keeping not only the secretary but also the president better informed and more involved with military decision making.

I also find interesting the idea that the chiefs have failed by not being able to look at the big picture when it comes to issues such as force levels, budget priorities and, therefore, do not make sound recommendations that consider all the services as a whole. Admiral Moorer answers this criticism perfectly:

> I cannot accept the proposed solution—to assign responsibility to a strengthened chairman—as a way of providing civilian decision makers with professional military advice. If "interservice rivalry" is so rampant, why should the chairman of the Joint Chiefs, who has been drawn from one of the services and most likely was serv-

ing as a member of the Joint Chiefs of Staff, suddenly change his position and produce the all-knowing, balanced force structure prior to his assignment as chairman?[34]

The Goldwater-Nichols Act is a distinct threat to civilian control of the military. Time will only make it worse. We are changing our system a great deal by making the chairman of the Joint Chiefs the most powerful military officer in our history, by creating a new powerful vice chairman out of nowhere, and by simultaneously strengthening the power of the unified and specified commanders around the world. Unfortunately, there has been little understanding, among the American people, of the effect these extensive changes will have on policy formation or military effectiveness.

I believe the new legislation is a mistake because:

- It does nothing to improve the effectiveness of the secretary of defense and to recognize his critical role in both peacetime and wartime.
- It goes against the political reality of the nuclear age as revealed in events since the start of the nuclear age.
- It does not consider the change in civilian involvement necessitated by the swiftness of modern communications.
- It assumes that all military problems are best solved by focusing on joint military operations while forgetting that the individual services form the critical base for all U.S. military activity.
- It goes against the crucial element of our form of government (civilian control of the military) and does not consider the need for civilian authority to control to varying degrees, depending on the situation, not only political policy but also strategy and implementation as well. This is precisely why, as General Vessey said, everything must revolve around the secretary of defense. President Eisenhower understood this need.

The fact is that nuclear weapons and the complexity of the modern world have made political grand strategy, as established by civilian leadership, no longer easily separated from military implementation. This reality was not used as the basis for the Goldwater-Nichols Act. What this legislation does is assume that a more powerful JCS chairman will somehow have all the answers. Our complex military cannot run well when any one military man has enough power to dominate events. We never want to be in a position where the president and the secretary of defense have to take into consideration not only what the JCS chairman recommends but also the fact of his power over the military establishment of the United States. One unelected military officer with vast military power could, over time, create a constitutional crisis by challenging civilian leadership or cause a disaster even greater than Vietnam.

What is needed are ways for making the military establishment truly responsive to the political goals of this nation. The best way to do this is to use my seven recommendations to improve the effectiveness of the key people in the system: the president and the secretary of defense. The method will insure civilian control of the military and military effectiveness as well. One-man military rule, which is the law now, must be changed before it is too late.

FOOTNOTES

CHAPTER I

[1]Goldwater-Nichols Defense Department Reorganization Act of 1986, 99th Congress, 2nd sess. Remarks by Congressman Les Aspin.

[2]Remarks by Congressman Les Aspin before a meeting of the American Stock Exchange, October 21, 1986, Washington, D.C.

[3]Staff report to the House Armed Services Committee on Defense Organization: The Need for Change, 1985, 99th Congress, 1st sess., p. 16.

[4]Goldwater-Nichols Act, 99th Congress, 2nd sess.

[5]Lyman L. Lemnitzer, "Retain the Joint Chiefs," *The New York Times,* June 1984, p. A27.

[6]Fleet Admiral Ernest J. King in hearing before the Senate Committee on Naval Affairs on Unification of the Armed Forces, 79th Congress, 2nd sess., ser. S2044, pt. 92925, on May 7, 1946.

[7]Goldwater-Nichols Act, 99th Congress, 2nd sess. Remarks by Congressman Les Aspin.

[8]Matthew B. Ridgway, *The Korean War* (Garden City, New York: Doubleday and Company, Inc., 1967), p. 232.

[9]Goldwater-Nichols Act, 99th Congress, 2nd sess.

[10]*Ibid.*

[11]Fleet Admiral Ernest J. King, "Admiral King Sees One-Man Power in Merger Plan," *New York Herald Tribune,* May 8, 1946.

[12]Lawrence J. Korb, "Service Unification: Arena of Fears, Hopes and Ironies," *Proceedings Naval Review* (Annapolis: U.S. Naval Institute Press, 1978), p. 182.

[13]Edward C. Meyer, "The JCS—How Much Reform Is Needed?," *Armed Forces Journal International,* April 1982, p. 88.

[14]Goldwater-Nichols Act, 99th Congress, 2nd sess.

[15]Bruce Palmer, Jr., *The Twenty-five Year War: America's Military Role in Vietnam* (Lexington, Kentucky: The University Press of Kentucky, 1984), p. 197.

[16]John H. Lehman, Jr. former navy secretary, telephone interview, New York, New York, March 1988.

[17]Statement of Admiral William J. Crowe, Jr., chairman of the Joint Chiefs of Staff, before the Senate Armed Services Committee on Defense Organization, 12 December 1985.

[18] Goldwater-Nichols Act, 99th Congress, 2nd sess.

[19] *Ibid.*

[20] *Ibid.*

[21] Admiral Matthew B. Ridgway, personal letter to Secretary of Defense Neil S. McElroy, February 6, 1958.

[22] General Thomas H. Moorer, "No Reorganization Required," *Washington Times,* May 13, 1985, p. 1D.

[23] Goldwater-Nichols Act, 99th Congress, 2nd sess.

[24] Korb, "Service Unification," p. 177.

[25] Goldwater-Nichols Act, 99th Congress, 2nd sess.

[26] King, "Admiral King Sees One-Man Power in Merger Plan," *New York Herald Tribune,* May 8, 1946.

[27] Goldwater-Nichols Act, 99th Congress, 2nd sess.

[28] Moorer, "No Reorganization Required," p. 1D.

[29] Admiral J. L. Holloway III, *Inside the JCS: Decisions in Crises* (Naval War College, Newport, Rhode Island: By the author, 1985), p. 16.

[30] Goldwater-Nichols Act, 99th Congress, 2nd sess.

[31] Holloway, *Inside the JCS,* p. 16.

[32] Palmer, Jr., *The Twenty-five Year War,* p. 18.

[33] Moorer, "No Reorganization Required," p. 1D.

[34] Robert S. Hirschfield, "The Scope and Limits of Presidential Power," in *Power and the Presidency,* eds. Philip C. Dolce and George H. Skau (New York: Charles Scribner's Sons, 1976), p. 293.

[35] *Ibid.,* p. 302.

[36] George Mason, speech at the Constitutional Convention, Philadelphia, Pennsylvania, 6 June 1787.

CHAPTER II

[1] James E. Hewes, Jr., *From Root to McNamara: Army Organization and Administration 1900–1963* (Washington, D.C.: U.S. Government Printing Office, Library of Congress No. 77-183069, 1974), p. 213.

[2] Ernest J. King and Walter Muir Whitehill, *A Naval Record* (New York: W. W. Norton and Company, Inc., 1952), p. 356.

[3] Samuel Eliot Morison, *History of the United States Naval Operations in World War II.*

[4] Lawrence J. Korb, "Service Unification: Arena of Fears, Hopes and Ironies," *Proceedings Naval Review* (Annapolis: U.S. Naval Institute Press, 1978), p. 175.

[5] Robert E. Sherwood, *Roosevelt and Hopkins* (New York: Harper and Row, Publishers Inc., 1948), p. 446.

[6] U.S. Department of Defense, Office of the Chief of Military History, U.S. Army, Superintendent of Documents, *Cross-Channel Attack,* by Gordon A. Harrison (Reprint ed., 1977), p. 92.

[7] William D. Leahy, *I Was There* (New York: McGraw-Hill, Inc., 1950), p. 106.

[8]Kent Roberts Greenfield, *American Strategy in World War II* (Baltimore: The Johns Hopkins University Press, 1963), p. 49.

[9]Hewes, *From Root to McNamara,* p. 58.

[10]E. B. Potter, *Bull Halsey* (Annapolis: U.S. Naval Institute Press, 1985), p. 267.

[11]*Ibid.,* p. 275.

[12]Richard F. Haynes, *The Awesome Power* (Baton Rouge: Louisiana State University Press, 1973), p. 12.

[13]Wilbur H. Morrison, *Above and Beyond* (New York: Bantam Books, Inc., 1983), p. 48.

[14]General Lord Ismay, *The Memoirs of General Lord Ismay* (New York: The Viking Press, 1960), p. 254.

CHAPTER III

[1]Richard F. Haynes, *The Awesome Power* (Baton Rouge: Louisiana State University Press, 1973), pp. 30–31.

[2]James McGovern, *To the Yalu* (New York: William Morrow and Company, Inc., 1972), p. 117.

[3]Robert J. Donovan, *Nemesis: Truman and Johnson in the Coils of War in Asia* (New York: St. Martin's/Marek, 1984), p. 14.

[4]Clay Blair, *The Forgotten War: America in Korea 1950–1953* (New York: Times Books, 1987), p. 29.

[5]Joseph C. Goulden, *Korea: The Untold Story of the War* (New York: Times Books, 1982), p. XVI.

[6]James F. Schnable, *Policy and Direction: The First Year* (Washington, D.C.: U.S. Government Printing Office, 1972), pp. 59–60.

[7]Matthew B. Ridgway, *Soldier: The Memoirs of Matthew B. Ridgway* (New York: Harper and Row, Publishers Inc., 1956), p. 191.

[8]Schnable, *Policy and Direction,* p. 66.

[9]*Ibid.,* p. 79.

[10]Goulden, *Korea: The Untold Story,* p. 67.

[11]*Ibid.,* p. 91.

[12]*Ibid.,* p. 138.

[13]Ridgway, *Soldier,* p. 222.

[14]Robert J. Donovan, *Tumultous Years: The Presidency of Harry S. Truman 1949–1953* (New York: W. W. Norton and Company, Inc., 1962), p. 361.

[15]Omar N. Bradley and Clay Blair, *A General's Life—An Autobiography* (New York: Simon and Schuster, 1983), p. 634.

[16]Goulden, *Korea: The Untold Story,* pp. 490.

[17]David S. McLellan, *Dean Acheson—The State Department Years* (New York: Dodd, Mead and Company, 1976), p. 313.

[18]Donovan, *Tumultous Years,* p. 362.

[19]Bradley and Blair, *A General's Life,* p. 634.

[20] Richard E. Neustadt and Ernest R. May, *Thinking in Time* (New York: The Free Press, 1986), p. 251.

[21] Walter Isaacson and Evan Thomas, *The Wise Men* (New York: Simon and Schuster, Inc., 1986), p. 537.

[22] John W. Spanier, *The Truman-MacArthur Controversy and the Korean War* (New York: W. W. Norton and Company, Inc., 1965), p. 6.

[23] *Ibid.*, p. 1.

[24] *Ibid.*, p. 77.

[25] *Ibid.*, pp. 123, 124.

[26] D. Clayton James, *Triumph and Disaster 1945–1964* (Boston: Houghton Mifflin Company, 1985), p. 499.

[27] *Ibid.*, pp. 499, 500.

[28] John W. Spanier, *The Truman-MacArthur Controversy*, p. 129.

[29] *Ibid.*, p. 235.

[30] Bernard Brodie, *War and Politics* (New York: MacMillan Publishing Company, 1973), p. 91.

CHAPTER IV

[1] James Coates and Michael Kilian, *Heavy Losses: The Dangerous Decline of American Defense* (New York: The Viking Press, 1985), p. 2.

[2] Graham T. Allison, *Essence of Decision* (Boston: Little, Brown and Company, 1971), p. 25.

[3] U.S. Department of Defense, Office of the Secretary of Defense, *The Department of Defense Documents on Establishment and Organization 1944–1978,* eds. Alice C. Cole, Alfred Goldberg, Samuel A. Tucker, and Rudolph A. Winnacker; Washington, D.C., 1978, p. 144.

[4] Alain C. Enthoven and K. Wayne Smith, *How Much Is Enough? Shaping the Defense Program, 1961–1969* (New York: Harper and Row, Publishers Inc., 1971), p. 10.

[5] Walter Isaacson and Evan Thomas, *The Wise Men* (New York: Simon and Schuster, Inc., 1986), p. 538.

[6] Clark A. Murdock, *Defense Policy Formation* (Albany: State University of N.Y. Press, 1974), p. 43.

[7] William Bragg Ewald, Jr., *Eisenhower the President: Crucial Days 1951–1960* (Englewood Cliffs, N.J.: Prentice-Hall, Inc., 1981), p. 192.

[8] Stephen Ambrose, *Eisenhower—The President* (New York: Simon and Schuster, Inc., 1984), pp. 223–224.

[9] Matthew B. Ridgway, *Soldier: The Memoirs of Matthew B. Ridgway* (New York: Harper and Row, Publishers Inc., 1956), p. 286.

[10] Maxwell Taylor, *The Uncertain Trumpet* (New York: Harper and Row, Publishers Inc., 1959), p. 5.

[11] Murdock, *Defense Policy Formation,* p. 14.

[12] Ewald, Jr., *Eisenhower the President,* p. 249.

[13] Taylor, *The Uncertain Trumpet,* p. 105.

[14] Robert Lackie, *The Wars of America* (New York: Harper and Row, Publishers Inc., 1981), p. 950.

[15] Maxwell Taylor, *Swords and Plowshares* (New York: W. W. Norton and Company, Inc., 1972), pp. 164–165.

[16] Russell P. Weigley, *The American Way of War* (New York: The MacMillan Publishing Company, 1973), p. 402.

[17] Anthony Leviero, "The Paradox That Is Admiral Radford," *The New York Times Magazine*, 5 August 1956, p. 11.

[18] Ewald, Jr., *Eisenhower the President,* p. 115.

[19] *Ibid.,* p. 119.

[20] *Ibid.,* p. 116.

[21] *Ibid.,* p. 118.

[22] Taylor, *Swords and Plowshares,* p. 171.

CHAPTER V

[1] Theodore C. Sorensen, *Kennedy* (New York: Harper and Row, Publishers Inc., 1968), p. 700.

[2] Maxwell Taylor, *Swords and Plowshares* (New York: W. W. Norton and Company, Inc., 1972), p. 274.

[3] Robert Kennedy, *Thirteen Days* (New York: W. W. Norton and Company, Inc., 1969), pp. 126–127.

[4] Charles Burton Marshall, *Cuba: Thoughts Prompted by the Crises—Washington, D.C.* (Washington, D.C.: Washington Center of Foreign Policy Research, no date), p. 3.

[5] Alexander L. George, *The Limits of Coercive Diplomacy* (Boston: Little, Brown and Company, 1971), p. 108.

[6] Graham T. Allison, *Essence of Decision* (Boston: Little, Brown and Company, 1971), p. 214.

[7] *Ibid.,* p. 127.

[8] *Ibid.,* p. 128.

[9] Elie Abel, *The Missile Crisis* (New York: Bantam Books, Inc., 1966), p. 57.

[10] Lawrence Korb, "George Whalen Anderson, Jr.," in *The Chiefs of Naval Operations,* ed. Robert William Love, Jr. (Annapolis: Naval Institute Press, 1980), p. 328.

[11] Allison, *Essence of Decision,* p. 128.

[12] George, *The Limits of Coercive Diplomacy,* p. 110.

[13] Abel, *The Missile Crisis,* p. 136.

[14] Taylor, *Swords and Plowshares,* p. 280.

CHAPTER VI

[1] Hearings before the Investigations Subcommittee of the Committee on Armed Services, House of Representatives, 98th Congress, 1st sess., June

14, 23, and 29, 1983, pp. 110, 224.

[2]*Ibid.*, p. 110.

[3]Bruce Palmer, Jr., *The Twenty-five-Year War: America's Military Role in Vietnam* (Lexington, Kentucky: The University Press of Kentucky, 1984), p. viii.

[4]Dave Richard Palmer, *Summons of the Trumpet: A History of the Vietnam War from a Military Viewpoint* (New York: Ballantine Books, 1978), p. 18.

[5]Caspar W. Weinberger, speech at the National Press Club, Washington, D.C., November 18, 1984.

[6]Fred C. Weyand and Harry G. Summers, Jr., "Vietnam Myths and American Realities," *Commanders Call,* July–August 1976, pp. 1–9.

[7]Hearings before the Investigations Subcommittee of the Committee on Armed Services, House of Representatives, 98th Congress, p. 117.

[8]Final report from the President's Blue Ribbon Commission on Defense Management, *A Quest for Excellence,* June, 1986, p. xvii.

[9]Roger Hilsman, *To Move a Nation* (Garden City, New York: Doubleday and Company, Inc., 1967), p. 411.

[10]Towsend Hoopes, *The Limits of Intervention: An Inside Account of How the Johnson Policy of Escalation in Vietnam Was Reversed* (New York: David McKay Company, Inc., 1969), pp. 68–69.

[11]William J. Rust, *Kennedy in Vietnam* (New York: Charles Scribner's Sons, 1985), p. 33.

[12]Chester L. Cooper, *The Lost Crusade: America in Vietnam* (New York: Dodd, Mead and Company, 1970), p. 422.

[13]Palmer, Jr., *The Twenty-five-Year War,* p. 177.

[14]Tristram Coffin, *Senator Fulbright: Portrait of a Public Philosopher* (New York: E. P. Dutton Inc., 1966), p. 283.

[15]Douglas Kinnard, *The War Managers* (Wayne, N.J.: Avery Publishing Group Inc., 1985), p. 46.

[16]Andrew F. Krepinevich, Jr., *The Army in Vietnam* (Baltimore: The Johns Hopkins University Press, 1986), p. 145.

[17]Robert J. Donovan, *Nemesis: Truman and Johnson in the Coils of War in Asia* (New York: St. Martin's/Marek, 1984), p. 96.

[18]Palmer, Jr., *The Twenty-five-Year War,* p. 43.

[19]Weinberger, speech at the National Press Club.

[20]Rust, *Kennedy in Vietnam,* p. 128.

[21]Palmer, Jr., *The Twenty-five-Year War,* p. 28.

[22]Hilsman, *To Move a Nation,* p. 411.

[23]Kinnard, *The War Managers,* p. 43.

[24]Walter Cronkite, television interview on September 2, 1963, *The New York Times,* September 3, 1963, p. 1:8.

[25]Maxwell Taylor, *Swords and Plowshares* (New York: W. W. Norton and Company, Inc., 1972), p. 400.

[26]Coffin, *Senator Fulbright,* p. 195.

[27]Hearings before the Investigations Subcommittee of the Committee on Armed Services, House of Representatives, 98th Congress, p. 106.

[28] Rust, *Kennedy in Vietnam,* p. 63.

[29] Harry G. Summers, Jr., *On Strategy, A Critical Analysis of the Vietnam War* (Novato, California: Presidio Press, 1982), p. 145.

[30] Hoopes, *The Limits of Intervention,* pp. 234–235.

[31] Krepinevich, Jr., *The Army in Vietnam,* p. 271.

[32] James Clay Thompson, *Rolling Thunder: Understanding Policy and Program Failure* (Chapel Hill: The University of North Carolina Press, 1980), pp. 10–11.

[33] Cooper, *The Lost Crusade,* p. 194.

[34] Weinberger, speech at the National Press Club.

[35] Eugene C. Windchy, *Tonkin Gulf* (New York: Doubleday and Company, Inc., 1971), p. 211.

[36] Weinberger, speech at the National Press Club.

[37] Cooper, *The Lost Crusade,* p. 62.

[38] Coffin, *Senator Fulbright,* p. 231.

[39] Palmer, *Summons of the Trumpet,* p. 34.

[40] Donovan, *Nemesis,* p. 96.

[41] *Ibid.,* p. 186.

[42] *Ibid.,* p. 67.

[43] Cooper, *The Lost Crusade,* p. 74.

[44] *Ibid.,* p. 107.

[45] *Ibid.,* p. 167.

[46] Palmer, Jr., *The Twenty-five-Year War,* p. 5.

[47] Kinnard, *The War Managers,* pp. 29, 30.

[48] Palmer, Jr., *The Twenty-five-Year War,* p. 9.

[49] Palmer, *Summons of the Trumpet,* p. 32.

[50] Coffin, *Senator Fulbright,* p. 234.

[51] Donovan, *Nemesis,* p. 29.

[52] Rust, *Kennedy in Vietnam,* p. IX.

[53] *Ibid.,* p. 34.

[54] Donovan, *Nemesis,* p. 64.

[55] Kinnard, *The War Managers,* p. 36.

[56] Hoopes, *The Limits of Intervention,* p. 104.

[57] Hearings before the Investigations Subcommittee of the Committee on Armed Services, House of Representatives, 98th Congress, p. 129.

[58] Palmer, Jr., *The Twenty-five-Year War,* p. 44.

[59] Hoopes, *The Limits of Intervention,* p. 62.

[60] Summers, Jr., *On Strategy,* p. 21.

[61] Palmer, Jr., *The Twenty-five-Year War,* p. 46.

[62] Donovan, *Nemesis,* pp. 10, 11.

[63] Hoopes, *The Limits of Intervention,* pp. 7, 8.

[64] Palmer, Jr., *The Twenty-five-Year War,* p. 87.

[65] Thompson, *Rolling Thunder,* pp. 29, 30.

[66] Hearings before the Investigations Subcommittee of the Committee on Armed Services, House of Representatives, 98th Congress, p. 121.

[67] Richard E. Neustadt, *Presidential Power: The Politics of Leadership* (New York: John Wiley and Sons, Inc., 1963), p. 128.

[68] Palmer, Jr., *The Twenty-five-Year War,* p. 193.

[69] Vermont Royster, "The Presidential Styles and the Churchill Model," *The Wall Street Journal,* January 7, 1987, p. 20.

[70] Summers, Jr., *On Strategy,* p. 63.

[71] Krepinevich, Jr., *The Army in Vietnam,* p. 164.

[72] Michael Dorman, "LBJ's '68 Decision," *Newsday,* March 27, 1988.

CHAPTER VII

[1] Harry G. Summers, Jr., *On Strategy, A Critical Analysis of the Vietnam War* (Novato, California: Presidio Press, 1982), p. XIV.

[2] John W. Spanier, *The Truman-MacArthur Controversy and the Korean War* (New York: W. W. Norton and Company, Inc., 1965), p. 279.

[3] Summers, Jr., *On Strategy,* p. 110.

[4] Staff Report to the House Armed Services Committee on Defense Organization: The Need for Change, 1985, 99th Congress, 1st sess., p. 44.

[5] Hearings before the Investigations Subcommittee of the Committee on Armed Services, House of Representatives, 98th Congress, 1st sess., June 14, 23, and 29, 1983, p. 121.

[6] Arthur T. Hadley, *The Straw Giant: Triumph and Failure—America's Armed Forces* (New York: Random House, Inc., 1986), p. 156.

[7] Testimony by Admiral James D. Watkins, chief of naval operations, before the Senate Armed Services Committee, 5 December 1985, 99th Congress, 1st sess.

[8] Fleet Admiral Ernest J. King, "Admiral King Hits a Single Command," *The New York Times,* February 18, 1946.

[9] Bruce Palmer, Jr., *The Twenty-five-Year War: America's Military Role in Vietnam,* (Lexington, Kentucky: The University Press of Kentucky, 1984), p. 199.

[10] Matthew B. Ridgway, *Soldier: The Memoirs of Matthew B. Ridgway* (New York: Harper and Row, Publishers Inc., 1956), p. 292.

[11] Andy Kerr, *A Journey Amongst the Good and the Great* (Annapolis: U.S. Naval Institute Press, 1987), p. 86.

[12] Palmer, Jr., *The Twenty-five-Year War,* p. 201.

[13] Testimony by Admiral James D. Watkins.

[14] Spanier, *The Truman-MacArthur Controversy,* p. 274.

[15] Admiral Matthew B. Ridgway, personal letter to Secretary of Defense Neil S. McElroy, February 6, 1958.

[16] Hearings before the Investigations Subcommittee of the Committee on Armed Services, House of Representatives, 99th Cong., 1st sess., June 13, 19 and 26, 1985, p. 204.

[17] Lawrence J. Korb, "Service Unification: Arena of Fears, Hopes and Ironies," *Proceedings Naval Review* (Annapolis: U.S. Naval Institute Press, 1978), p. 177.

[18] Les Aspin, "Rift Seen Between Reagan, Joint Chiefs," *Washington Post,* November 25, 1986, p. A14.

[19] Palmer, Jr., *The Twenty-five-Year War,* p. 202.

[20] John L. Frisbee, "New Life for JCS at Forty," *Air Force Magazine,* February, 1982, p. 88.

[21] U.S. Department of Defense, Office of the Secretary of Defense, *The Department of Defense Documents on Establishment and Organization 1944–1978,* eds. Alice C. Cole, Alfred Goldberg, Samuel A. Tucker, and Rudolph A. Winnacker; Washington, D.C., 1978, p. 176.

[22] Hearings before the Investigations Subcommittee of the Committee on Armed Services, House of Representatives, 98th Congress, 1st sess., June 14, 23, and 29, 1983, p. 79.

[23] *Ibid.,* p. 74.

[24] *Ibid.,* p. 127.

[25] *Ibid.,* p. 79.

[26] Palmer, Jr., *The Twenty-five-Year War,* pp. 198, 199.

[27] J. Brian Atwood, "Sharing War Powers," *The New York Times,* October 14, 1987, p. A35.

[28] Edward C. Meyer, "The JCS—How Much Reform Is Needed?," *Armed Forces Journal International,* April 1982, p. 82.

[29] Hearings before the Investigations Subcommittee of the Committee on Armed Services, House of Representatives, 98th Congress, p. 79.

[30] Final report from the president's Blue Ribbon Commission on Defense Management. *A Quest for Excellence,* June 1986.

[31] Hearings before the Investigations Subcommittee of the Committee on Armed Services, House of Representatives, 98th Congress, p. 71.

[32] *Ibid.,* p. 120.

[33] Maxwell Taylor, *The Uncertain Trumpet* (New York: Harper and Row, Publishers Inc., 1959), p. 95.

[34] Admiral Thomas H. Moorer, "No Reorganization Required," *Washington Times,* May 13, 1985, p. 1D.

BIBLIOGRAPHY

Abel, Elie, *The Missile Crisis*. New York: Bantam Books, Inc., 1966.

Allison, Graham T., *Essence of Decision*. Boston: Little, Brown and Company, 1971.

Ambrose, Stephen E., *Eisenhower—The President*. New York: Simon & Schuster, Inc., 1984.

———, *Eisenhower—Soldier, General of the Army, President-Elect 1890–1952*. New York: Simon and Schuster, Inc., 1983.

Aspin, Les, "Rift Seen Between Reagan, Joint Chiefs." *The Washington Post*, November 25, 1986.

Atwood, J. Brian, "Sharing War Powers." *The New York Times*, October 14, 1987.

Borklund, C. W., *The Department of Defense*. New York: Praeger Publishers, 1968.

Bradley, Omar N.; and Blair, Clay, *A General's Life—An Autobiography*. New York: Simon and Schuster, Inc., 1983.

Brodie, Bernard, *War and Politics*. New York: MacMillan Publishing Company, 1973.

Buell, Thomas B., *Master of Sea Power—A Biography of Fleet Admiral Ernest J. King*. Boston: Little, Brown and Company, 1980.

———, *The Quiet Warrior: A Biography of Admiral Raymond A. Spruance*. Boston: Little, Brown and Company, 1974.

Cardwell, Thomas A. III, *Command Structure for Theatre Warfare—The Quest for Unity of Command*. Washington, D.C.: U.S. Government Printing Office, 1984.

Coffin, Tristram, *Senator Fulbright: Portrait of a Public Philosopher*. New York: E. P. Dutton Inc., 1966.

Cole, Alice C.; Goldberg, Alfred; Tucker, Samuel A.; and Winnacker, Rudolf A., eds., *The Department of Defense Documents on Establishment and Organization 1944–1978*. Washington, D.C.: Office of the Secretary of Defense, 1978.

Collins, J. Lawton, *Lightning Joe*. Baton Rouge: Louisiana State University Press, 1979.

———, *War in Peacetime*. Boston: Houghton Mifflin Company, 1969.

Cooper, Chester L., *The Lost Crusade: America in Vietnam*. New York: Dodd, Mead and Company, 1970.

Donovan, Robert J., *Nemesis: Truman and Johnson in the Coils of War in Asia*. New York: St. Martin's/Marek, 1984.

———, *Tumultous Years: The Presidency of Harry S. Truman 1949–1953.* New York: W. W. Norton and Company, Inc., 1962.

Enthoven, Alain C.; and Smith, K. Wayne, *How Much Is Enough? Shaping the Defense Program.* New York: Harper and Row, Publishers Inc., 1971.

Ewald, William Bragg, Jr., *Eisenhower the President: Crucial Days 1951–1960.* Englewood Cliffs, N.J.: Prentice-Hall, Inc., 1981.

Fleming, Karl, "The Troubled Army Brass." *Newsweek,* May 24, 1971.

Forrestal, E. P., *Admiral Raymond A. Spruance: A Study in Command.* Washington, D.C.: U.S. Government Printing Office, 1966.

Gabriel, Richard A., *Military Incompetence: Why the American Military Doesn't Work.* New York: Hill and Wang, 1985.

George, Alexander L., *The Limits of Coercive Diplomacy.* Boston: Little, Brown and Company, 1971.

Goulden, Joseph C., *Korea: The Untold Story of the War.* New York: Times Books, 1982.

Greenfield, Kent Roberts, *American Strategy in World War II.* Baltimore: The Johns Hopkins University Press, 1963.

———, ed., *Command Decisions.* Washington, D.C.: Office of the Chief of Military History, United States Army, 1960; reprint ed., Washington, D.C.: U.S. Government Printing Office, 1971.

Hadley, Arthur T., *The Straw Giant: Triumph and Failure—America's Armed Forces.* New York: Random House, Inc., 1986.

Harrison, Gordon A., *Cross-Channel Attack.* Reprint ed., Washington, D.C.: Office of the Chief of Military History, U.S. Army. Superintendent of Documents, 1977.

Hayes, Grace Person, *The History of the Joint Chiefs of Staff in World War II.* Annapolis: U.S. Naval Institute Press, 1982.

Haynes, Richard F., *The Awesome Power.* Baton Rouge: Louisiana State University Press, 1973.

Hewes, James E., *From Root to McNamara: Organization and Administration 1900–1963.* Washington, D.C.: U.S. Government Printing Office, 1974.

Hilsman, Roger, *To Move a Nation.* New York: Doubleday and Company, Inc., 1967.

Hirschfield, Robert S., "The Scope and Limits of Presidential Power." In *Power and the Presidency,* p. 293. Edited by Philip C. Dolce and George H. Skau. New York: Charles Scribner's Sons, 1976.

Holloway, J. L. III, *Inside the JCS: Decisions in Crises.* Naval War College, Newport, Rhode Island: By the author, 1985.

Hoopes, Towsend, *The Limits of Intervention: An Inside Account of How the Johnson Policy of Escalation in Vietnam Was Reversed.* New York: David McKay Company, Inc., 1969.

Isaacson, Walter; and Thomas, Evan, *The Wise Men.* New York: Simon and Schuster, Inc., 1986.

James, D. Clayton, *Triumph and Disaster 1945–1964.* Boston: Houghton Mifflin Company, 1985.

Kennedy, Robert, *Thirteen Days*. New York: W. W. Norton and Company, Inc., 1969.

Kerr, Andy. *A Journey Amongst the Good and the Great*. Annapolis: U.S. Naval Institute Press, 1987.

King, Ernest J.; and Whitehill, Walter Muir, *Fleet Admiral Ernest J. King*. New York: W. W. Norton and Company, Inc., 1952.

Kinnard, Douglas, *The War Managers*. Wayne, N.J.: Avery Publishing Group Inc., 1985.

Korb, Lawrence, "George Whalen Anderson, Jr." In *The Chiefs of Naval Operations,* pp. 328–329. Edited by Robert William Love, Jr. Annapolis: U.S. Naval Institute Press, 1980.

———, *The Fall and Rise of the Pentagon*. Westport, Connecticut: Greenwood Press, 1979.

———, *The Joint Chiefs of Staff—The First Twenty-Five Years*. Bloomington: Indiana University Press, 1976.

———, "Service Unification: Arena of Fears, Hopes and Ironies." *Proceedings Naval Review.* Annapolis: U.S. Naval Institute Press, 1978.

Krepinevich, Andrew F., Jr., *The Army in Vietnam*. Baltimore: The Johns Hopkins University Press, 1986.

Lackie, Robert, *The Wars of America*. New York: Harper and Row, Publishers Inc., 1981.

Leahy, William D., *I Was There*. New York: McGraw-Hill, Inc., 1950.

Leviero, Anthony, "The Paradox That Is Admiral Radford." *New York Times Magazine,* August 5, 1955, p. 11.

MacGregor, James Burns, *Roosevelt: The Soldier of Freedom*. New York: Harcourt Brace Jovanovich, Inc., 1970.

Marshall, Charles Burton, *Cuba: Thoughts Prompted by the Crises*. Washington, D.C.: Washington Center of Foreign Policy Research, no date.

Mason, George, speech at the Constitutional Convention. Philadelphia, Pennsylvania, June 6, 1787.

Matloff, Maurice; and Snell, Edwin M., *Strategic Planning for Coalition Warfare 1941–1942*. Reprint ed., Washington, D.C.: U.S. Government Printing Office, 1970.

McGovern, James, *To the Yalu*. New York: William Morrow and Company, Inc., 1972.

McLellan, David S., *Dean Acheson—The State Department Years*. New York: Dodd, Mead and Company, 1976.

Meyer, Edward C., "The JCS—How Much Reform Is Needed?" In *Armed Forces Journal International,* April 1982.

Morison, Samuel Eliot, *History of the United States Naval Operations in World War II*.

Morrison, Wilbur H., *Above and Beyond*. New York: Bantam Books, Inc., 1983.

Morton, Louis, *The War in the Pacific, Strategy and Command the First Two Years*. Office of the Chief of Military History, Department of the Army. Washington, D.C.: U.S. Government Printing Office, 1969.

Murdock, Clark A., *Defense Policy Formation*. Albany: State University of New York Press, 1974.

Neustadt, Richard E.; and May, Ernest R., *Thinking in Time*. New York: The Free Press, 1986.

———, *Presidential Power: The Politics of Leadership*. New York: John Wiley and Sons, Inc., 1963.

Palmer, Bruce, Jr., *The Twenty-five-Year War: America's Military Role in Vietnam*. Lexington, Kentucky: The University Press of Kentucky, 1984.

Paper, Lewis J., *John F. Kennedy—The Promise and the Performance*. New York: Da Capo Press, Inc., 1975.

Pfannes, Charles E.; and Salamune, Victor A., *The Great Admirals of World War II*. Vol. 1: *The Americans*. New York: Kensington Publishing Corp., 1983.

Pogue, Forrest C., *George C. Marshall—Ordeal and Hope 1939–1942*. New York: The Viking Press, 1965, 1966.

Potter, E. B., *Bull Halsey*. Annapolis: U.S. Naval Institute Press, 1985.

Prange, Gordon W., *At Dawn We Slept: The Untold Story of Pearl Harbor*. New York: McGraw-Hill, Inc., 1981.

Reardon, Steven L., *The Formative Years 1947–1950*. History of the Office of the Secretary of Defense. Edited by Alfred Goldberg. Washington, D.C.: U.S. Government Printing Office, 1984.

Ridgway, Matthew B., *The Korean War*. New York: Doubleday and Company, Inc., 1967.

———, *Soldier: The Memoirs of Matthew B. Ridgway*. New York: Harper and Row, Publishers Inc., 1956.

Rogow, Arnold A., *James Forrestal: A Study of Personality, Politics and Policy*. New York: MacMillan Publishing Company, 1963.

Rust, William J., *Kennedy in Vietnam*. New York: Charles Scribner's Sons, 1985.

Ryan, Paul B., *The Iranian Rescue Mission: Why It Failed*. Annapolis: U.S. Naval Institute Press, 1985.

Schlesinger, Arthur M., Jr., *A Thousand Days. John F. Kennedy in the White House*. Boston: Houghton Mifflin Company, 1965.

Schnable, James F., *Policy and Direction: The First Year*. Washington, D.C.: U.S. Government Printing Office, 1972.

Sherwood, Robert E., *Roosevelt and Hopkins*. New York: Harper and Row, Publishers Inc., 1948.

Smith, Steve and Clark, Michael, eds., *Foreign Policy Implementation*. London: George Allen and Unwin, 1985.

Sorensen, Theodore C., *Kennedy*. New York: Harper and Row, Publishers Inc., 1968.

Spanier, John W., *The Truman-MacArthur Controversy and the Korean War*. New York: W. W. Norton and Company, Inc., 1965.

Spector, Ronald H., *Eagle Against the Sun: The American War with Japan*. New York: The Free Press, 1985.

Summers, Harry G., Jr., *On Strategy, A Critical Analysis of the Vietnam War.* Novato, California: Presidio Press, 1982.

Taylor, Maxwell, *Swords and Plowshares.* New York: W. W. Norton and Company, 1972.

———, *The Uncertain Trumpet.* New York: Harper and Row, Publishers Inc., 1959.

Thompson, James Clay, *Rolling Thunder: Understanding Policy and Program Failure.* Chapel Hill: The University of North Carolina Press, 1980.

Watson, Mark Skinner, *The War Department—Chief of Staff: Prewar Plans and Preparations.* Reprinted ed., Washington, D.C.: U.S. Government Printing Office, 1974.

Weigley, Russell P., *The American Way of War.* New York: MacMillan Publishing Company, 1973.

———, *Eisenhower's Lieutenants—The Campaign of France and Germany 1944–1945.* Bloomington: Indiana University Press, 1981.

Whitehill, Walter Muir; and King, Ernest J., *A Naval Record.* New York: W. W. Norton and Company, Inc., 1952.

Windchy, Eugene G., *Tonkin Gulf.* New York: Doubleday and Company, Inc., 1971.

Wyden, Peter, *Bay of Pigs.* New York: Simon and Schuster, Inc., 1979.

Index